"It is incumbent upon each generation of would-be Protestants to reaffirm and restate the biblical basis and ongoing relevance of the Reformation's theological legacy. In this slender but substantial volume, Davy Ellison makes the case afresh that the five Reformation solas are vital, not just for understanding our sixteenth-century heritage, but for understanding how the Triune God is still at work in the church and world today."

Dr. Matthew C. Bingham
Lecturer in Systematic Theology and Church History,
Oak Hill College, London

"Modern evangelicalism suffers with doctrinal anemia. Pastors and church leaders are often obsessed with theological fads or pragmatic church growth practices that lead to theologically weak churches with shallow discipleship. What evangelicals need is a reinvigorated understanding of Scripture, the gospel, and the glory of God. By surveying the five Solas of the Reformation, Davy Ellison reminds us of glorious gospel truths and how they should shape our lives. This book unfolds the most essential and important truths of the Christian faith and provides compelling, rich application of those truths to both individual Chr

Dr. Sam Em
Senior Editor

"The Reformation was a mig   ospel truths were recovered for the vitality of God's church. This book provides a helpful introductory window into five of these beautiful truths and should thus be a great help to many."

Rev. Dr. Mark Earngey
Lecturer in Christian Thought,
Moore Theological College, Sydney, Australia

"This little book introduces in an accessible way some key themes of the Reformation under the rubric of the five solas. Each sola is covered biblically and historically with insightful practical applications. Written at a popular level, *Five: The Solas of the Reformation* will encourage Christians in their spiritual lives and inspire further reflection on a pivotal period of church history. More importantly, in these pages Davy Ellison has captured the essence of the Christian gospel and in the process of better informing doctrinal convictions, has challenged the contemporary church to leave a faithful legacy for future generations."

Edwin Ewart

Principal, Irish Baptist College, Northern Ireland

"Our contemporary culture doesn't really like to use the word alone. We don't like exclusive claims. And yet Davy Ellison shows us how beautiful it is to understand five ways this word alone secures true redemption. Travel with him through history and God's word to delight in what alone will bring you joy today."

Aimee Byrd

Author of *No Little Women* and *Theological Fitness*, cohost of *Mortification of Spin*

"Five hundred years ago, Christians across Europe turned to their Bibles to find out what had happened to God's good news. They set out to untangle the church that they loved from the confusions of its history. In doing so, they summarised their message in five great claims. In explaining what these claims mean, Davy Ellison's new book will introduce a new generation of readers to the things that matter most."

Dr. Crawford Gribben

Professor of Early-Modern British History, Queen's University Belfast, Northern Ireland

"Ellison collaborates with a chorus of voices from the past to clarify and illustrate truths that Christians have held dear for hundreds of years. This primer on the five solas is no dry history lesson, but is relevant to every believer. Many of us have our lives shaken by the storms of theological controversies, sin struggles, or recurring doubts, and we need to be reminded that our faith has a solid foundation."

> **Gloria Furman**
>
> Author of *Treasuring Christ When Your Hands Are Full* and *Missional Motherhood*

"For those unfamiliar with the Reformation this serves as a useful primer by introducing the 'Solas', the big five ideas, that emerged from it. It does so in a non-technical way while showing how these are rooted in Scripture and have important contemporary implications."

> **Dr. David Luke**
>
> Tutor in Historical Theology and Church History,
> Irish Baptist College, Northern Ireland

FIVE
The Solas of the Reformation

S. D. Ellison

Five: The Solas of the Reformation
Copyright © 2020 by S. D. Ellison

All rights reserved. Except for brief quotations in critical publications, reviews or as may be permitted by the Copyright Act, no part of this book may be used or reproduced in any manner whatsoever without prior written permission from the publisher.

Scripture quotations are from The ESV® Bible (The Holy Bible, English Standard Version®), copyright © 2001 by Crossway, a publishing ministry of Good News Publishers. Used by permission. All rights reserved.

For information contact:
Tulip Publishing, PO Box 3150, Lansvale, NSW, Australia 2166
www.tulippublishing.com.au

Book and Cover design by Tulip Publishing

PAPERBACK ISBN: 978-0-6485399-7-1
DIGITAL ISBN: 978-0-6485399-8-8

10 9 8 7 6 5 4 3 2 1

For John and Lourdes Brew
In gratitude for your example of missionary zeal.
In recognition of your faithfulness in upholding these truths in Peru.

CONTENTS

ACKNOWLEDGEMENTS		XI
FOREWORD		XIII
INTRODUCTION		1
1. SOLA SCRIPTURA	*Scripture alone*	5
2. SOLA GRATIA	*Grace alone*	21
3. SOLA FIDE	*Faith alone*	37
4. SOLUS CHRISTUS	*Christ alone*	55
5. SOLI DEO GLORIA	*Glory to God alone*	71
CONCLUSION		89
ENDNOTES		91

ACKNOWLEDGEMENTS

This book began life as a series of lectures delivered in Tacna, Peru in October 2017. These lectures were organised to mark the 500th anniversary of the Reformation. I found myself in Tacna with the task of teaching on the Five Solas at the invitation of John Brew. If it had not been for John's invitation it is unlikely that this material would have existed. Additionally, if it had not been for his invitation I would not have had the delight of Lourdes' hospitality. Lourdes' pork remains unsurpassed. With love and admiration I gladly dedicate this book to you both for your example in missionary zeal and faithfulness to Scripture.

Baptist Missions, and in particular Mervyn Scott and Joanne Dunstan, deserve mention. Their encouragement and kindness in facilitating my trip to Peru made the organisation simpler than it may have been otherwise. A visit to Peru in 2006 was instrumental in my conversion. Therefore, it was particularly poignant to be afforded the opportunity to return in 2017, especially with the privilege of teaching the Scriptures. My gratitude to Mervyn for assisting with this visit is deep.

Writing is a process. This process is always aided by input from beyond the author. This I received from Bríd Morton and Matthew Kelso. In the midst of busy lives they kindly worked their way through earlier drafts of this book. Bríd and Matthew, your perceptive comments and suggestions have made me a better writer, and your timely encouragements have kept me writing. Thank you for your help. I must also thank Brett Lee-Price and Tulip Publishing for taking a risk with an unknown author. The skill and professionalism exhibited in guiding this material to publication is much appreciated. May God continue to raise up those with a desire to supply Christians with good books.

I have said it many times, but it is worth repeating: without my wife's help and support I would never have enjoyed the same opportunity to study, preach, teach, and write. Tracy is tireless in her encouragement and constant in her love. Truly the best companion of my life. I praise God for such a partner in life, love, and ministry. I trust you feel as cherished as you are.

None of this would be possible without the Scriptures, which are able to make us wise for salvation. This they do by proclaiming salvation by grace alone, through faith alone, in Christ alone. It is only because of this salvation that I have any interest in these truths. Therefore, all of the glory is God's, and his alone.

FOREWORD

As a church historian, I am always thrilled to find Christians who take history seriously. That is far from being the norm today in the breadth of what used to be called Christendom. Many use history as an entertaining diversion. I am thinking here of the enormous popularity of Christian historical fiction, some of which is really good, but most of which has as much claim to being fine literature as Harlequin romances. And yes, preachers will often use history to make sermonic points, but far too frequently do so without attention to context and the complexity of historical narrative. So, I was doubly delighted to find this primer on the core issues of the sixteenth-century Reformation, namely, the five solas, setting them in their original historical context and doing so responsibly. In addition to this, Davy Ellison shows how each of them is grounded in the Scriptures, thus illustrating the Reformation emphasis on taking its guidance first and foremost from Holy Scripture.

Then, this is a primer, that is, an introduction to these great theological truths. Recently, another publisher issued five books on this subject: one for each sola. Those were truly in-depth studies of these most needful theological affirmations. This book, on the other hand, is a first introduction to all five of the solas and, as such, is both brief and to the point. But Mr. Ellison has been able to accomplish this without compromising the awesomeness of these doctrines. It was the remarkable North African pastor-theologian Augustine (beloved by all of the Reformers) who once said that holy Scripture has riches deep enough that an elephant could launch into its waters, as it were, and never touch bottom. But it was simple enough for a small lamb to come down to its shores and lap water and be refreshed and even swim to its heart's content and have no fear of drowning. Well, such is true of these doctrines: deep enough to fill five volumes, and yet, basic enough for a first-rate primer like this.

Michael A.G. Haykin, FRHistS
Chair and Professor of Church History
The Southern Baptist Theological Seminary.

INTRODUCTION
Reverberations from the Sixteenth Century

Have you ever paused to consider the extent to which your daily life is influenced by history? Our lives are irrefutably shaped by the events of history. Whether positively or negatively, we are all products of our past. This is true individually, nationally, and globally. Histories converge, and as they do so they produce the present. This reality is no less true in the realm of theology. As Stephen J. Wellum, Professor of Christian Theology at the Southern Baptist Theological Seminary, puts it:

> Beyond question, the Protestant Reformation of the 16th Century changed Christianity forever. The Reformation was not perfect, but it was a mighty reviving movement of the Spirit of God which purified the Church and called people back to the fundamentals of the Gospel.[1]

In modern Christianity this statement, at best, will be met with a mixed response. Some will reject it outright, others will seek to temper it, and those in the Reformed camp might stretch to a hallelujah and an amen! While Wellum's claim might be startling, it is no overstatement.

The events of sixteenth century Europe continue to reverberate throughout the Protestant Church. Indeed, throughout society at large, especially in Europe and the United States of America. It is because of these continued reverberations that we remain both interested in what took place and indebted to the truths that (re-) emerged in the sixteenth century. Even though it is more than five hundred years since Martin Luther unknowingly set in motion what would become known as *The Reformation*, we continue to stand in its shadow. We are products of this past.

The truths that re-emerged during the Reformation dictate the content of this book. Although it wasn't until the twentieth century that what we now know as the *Five Solas* were systematised, their content is clearly discernible in the writings of the Reformers. These truths are often expressed in Latin slogans: *Sola Scriptura* (Scripture Alone), *Sola Gratia* (Grace Alone), *Sola Fide* (Faith Alone), *Solus Christus* (Christ Alone), and *Soli Deo Gloria* (Glory to God Alone). These Latin slogans crisply capture the theological convictions that underpinned the Reformation. We will devote one chapter to each slogan, and each chapter will follow a similar pattern of exploring the Reformers' contribution, examining Scripture to test the Reformers' arguments, and finally I offer a few principles for application today. Some may be disappointed that I do not quote the Reformers from original sources. This was an intentional decision in order to introduce the reader to a wider array of secondary literature on the *Five Solas*. This material is not primarily for the pastor and theologian, but for every Christian.

I am convinced that a deepening understanding of the truths that re-emerged during the Reformation, and a firmer adherence to them, will lead to a more faithful Church. Just as in centuries gone by, so too today Christianity faces many challenges. These challenges arise from both within and without. It will be impossible to resolutely face the subtle challenges from within the Church and the explicit challenges from a hostile world outside the Church without a firm foundation. The *Five Solas* offer us that necessary foundation. A firm foundation in the Triune God, who in love has acted to rescue his people, and has communicated this message in his word. By God's grace, may these reverberations from the sixteenth century cause Christ's Church to be purified in the present by calling us back to the fundamentals of the gospel.

1

SOLA SCRIPTURA
Scripture Alone

Scripture's Power and Beauty[1]

The city was notorious for violence. Gambling was rife. Entertainment consisted of provocative dancing, drunkenness, and, perhaps unsurprisingly, sexual immorality. The citizens would often parade the city streets naked while singing vulgar songs. God was roundly dishonoured in both word and deed. All of this was an embarrassment to those who governed early sixteenth century Catholic Geneva, Switzerland.

As they attempted to restrain this behaviour, the governing council of Geneva, the Council of Two Hundred, took increasingly drastic action. To begin with, the council passed various laws, hoping that legislation would remedy the problem. However, in the face of mere legislation, the decline in Geneva's morals continued unabated. The council also decided to break with Catholicism and align the city with the Protestant Reformation. This was not a theological decision, but a desperate attempt to curb the wild behaviour of Geneva's citizens. Finally, the council extended an invitation to a man named John Calvin to become Geneva's Chief Pastor.

In August 1536, Calvin arrived in Geneva. It was quite an unspectacular beginning to his ministry. Calvin found himself roundly ignored by both the city at large, and the council who had invited him. Worse still, he was not paid for his first year of work. After serving for less than two years, in 1538, he was dismissed from his position. Circumstances in Geneva continued to deteriorate, and so once again, the city turned to Calvin. Given his initial experience, Calvin was understandably reluctant to return. Yet, out of a sense of duty, he eventually agreed.

Come September 1541, Calvin found himself in the city of Geneva once more. In returning to Geneva, he returned to his main weapon against the lude behaviour he had previously observed – the Bible. In fact, he resumed preaching from the very place that he had finished in 1538. Every day, Calvin preached from the Bible. Slowly, but surely, and as biblical knowledge increased, people were convicted of their sin and underwent a moral transformation by the power of God. The city cared for the poor and unwanted. Education was provided for all classes of people. Industry was developed. True liberty was enjoyed. Remarkably, at least in the historian's eyes, this was accomplished by one man simply preaching the Bible.

This brief history of John Calvin's arrival in Geneva illustrates powerfully the Reformation cry of *Sola Scriptura*—Scripture Alone. Indeed, it illustrates the power and the beauty of Scripture. In what follows, we will observe this power and beauty of Scripture in the thinking of the Reformers and the pages of Scripture. We will then end this chapter by considering how the Reformation cry of *Sola Scriptura* is relevant for us today.

The Authority of this Power and Beauty

It is important to highlight that the primary issue underlying the Reformation was not the issue of justification, but the issue of authority. Martin Luther's complaint against the Catholic Church was, first and foremost, their claim to final authority. It just so happened that justification was the avenue through which the issue was most starkly demonstrated. This becomes apparent as we consider Luther's view of Scripture.

Martin Luther: Captive to the Word of God

The Catholic Church of the sixteenth century held to a two-source theory of authority: Scripture *and* Tradition. Seedlings of this kind of thinking can be traced back to the fourth century. It can be discerned in the work of the early Church Fathers, such as John Chrysostom, Basil and Augustine. These seedlings developed into saplings during the twelfth century. And, largely due to the writings of the canon lawyers, this two-source theory of authority became more explicit and widespread. These saplings matured further in the fourteenth century through the writings of William of Ockham. Therefore, by the sixteenth century, it was firmly established that Scripture and Tradition were to be considered equally authoritative and supplementary sources of divine revelation.[2] This two-source theory of authority was finally confirmed by the Council of Trent in the Counter-Reformation. This council met three times between December 1545 and December 1563 in an attempt to combat Reformation teaching that was circulating throughout Europe.

Surprisingly, Luther's view of Scripture is not explicitly expressed in his 95 Theses, famously nailed to the Wittenberg Church door in 1517. Instead, Luther's view was made explicit as a result of three debates which took place in light of the *95 Theses*. Here Luther's view of Scripture emerged as being at odds with the position of the Catholic Church. Initially, Luther faced Sylvester (Mazzolini) Prierias, a Dominican theologian, drafted in by Pope Leo X to respond to Luther's position. Prierias quickly discerned that the issue at stake was one of authority. This was followed by a debate between Luther and Cardinal Cajetan in October 1518. However, Luther's toughest challenge came in 1519 when he faced the well-known theologian, Johannes von Eck, on the issue of authority. These three debates made it abundantly clear that Luther viewed Scripture *alone* as the final authority.[3] As one historian notes, the stronger the argument for the Papacy's infallibility, the more Luther relied on the Scriptures.[4]

These debates did not settle the matter. As the dispute continued, Luther's position crystallised, leading to the clarity in Luther's famous statement delivered at the Diet of Worms in 1521. When asked to recant all that he had written on the subject, Luther replied:

> Unless I am convinced by the testimony of the Scriptures or by clear reason…I am bound by the Scriptures I have quoted and my conscience is captive to the Word of God. I cannot and I will not retract anything, since it is neither safe nor right to go against conscience. I cannot do otherwise, here I stand, may God help me.[5]

It is apparent, then, that "[I]n Martin Luther's day, *sola Scriptura* had to do with the Bible being the sole authority for Christians over against challenges to it from the traditions of the medieval church, church councils, and the popes. The reformers wanted Scripture to stand alone as the Church's true authority."[6] Martin Luther was captive to the Word of God.

Ulrich Zwingli and John Calvin: Devoted to Scripture

Luther was not alone. Others, recognising and accepting the Reformation cry of *Sola Scriptura,* were also captive to the Word of God. Ulrich Zwingli, a contemporary of Luther, led the Reformation in Zurich, Switzerland. Zwingli was convicted under the principle of *Sola Scriptura* to abandon the prescribed lectionary of the day. Rather than following the set readings of the Church week-by-week, Zwingli devoted himself to preach verse-by-verse through whole books of the Bible.[7]

This verse-by-verse exposition, as we have observed above, was also John Calvin's practice. Calvin was part of the second generation of the Reformers. By the time he was writing, the cry of *Sola Scriptura* had continued to develop and mature in Reformation thinking. This is particularly evident in his *Institutes of the Christian Religion*, where Calvin is scathing of the Catholic Church and their continued defence of a two-source theory of authority. In Calvin's mind, to argue that ultimate authority may be derived from human tradition as well as Scripture is despicable. He writes:

> Now daily oracles are not sent from heaven, for it pleased the Lord to hallow his truth to everlasting remembrance in the Scriptures alone... But a pernicious error widely prevails that Scripture has only so much weight as is conceded to it by the consent of the church. As if the eternal and inviolable truth of God depended upon the decision of man![8]

Zwingli and Calvin were devoted to the Word of God. They believed it, submitted to it and preached it.

Defining Sola Scriptura

There is no single, definitive, statement on *Sola Scriptura* from the Reformers. Rather, there is a clear understanding of Scripture as the sole authority for the Christian and the Church, which was later termed *Sola Scriptura*. It is incumbent upon us, then, to attempt to define exactly what the Reformers understood of Scripture. What were the key components in their doctrine of Scripture?

In light of 2 Timothy 3:16–17 (ESV), "All Scripture is breathed out by God and profitable for teaching, for reproof, for correction, and for training in righteousness, that the man of God may be competent, equipped for every good work", the Reformers understood God's Word to be inspired, inerrant, and sufficient. These three elements were the key components to the Reformers' doctrine of Scripture.

Unlike theological discussion today, there wasn't much of a debate regarding the inspiration of Scripture in the sixteenth century. Both the Catholic Church and the Protestant Reformers believed the Bible to be divinely inspired. The Reformers, however, logically reasoned if Scripture is inspired by God, it must be inerrant. Matthew Barrett helpfully explains Luther's logic on this:

> [I]t is important for us to note that for Luther sola scriptura was directly connected to the inerrancy of Scripture. Luther did not use the term 'inerrancy' in his writings or in debate, yet the concept is present throughout his thinking on the matter. If Scripture is not inerrant, then sola scriptura is without a foundation. For Luther, what made the Bible alone the supreme authority was that it was not only inspired by God but as a result of being God-breathed the Scriptures, and the Scriptures alone, could not and do not err. On the other hand, church councils and popes can and do err. So while Rome believed Scripture and Tradition were inerrant authorities, Luther argued that Scripture alone is our inerrant authority from God.[9]

The Reformers asserted that as Scripture comes from God, it must subsequently be without error.

In addition to this, the Reformers argued that Scripture is also sufficient—it is all we need. This is summarised by John MacArthur:

> The Reformation principle of sola Scriptura has to do with the sufficiency of Scripture as our supreme authority in all spiritual matters. Sola Scriptura simply means that all truth necessary for our salvation and spiritual life is taught either explicitly or implicitly in Scripture. It is not a claim that all truth of every kind is found in Scripture... [Rather] Scripture is the highest and supreme authority on any matter on which it speaks.[10]

In other words, "everything necessary, everything binding on our conscience, and everything God requires of us is given to us in Scripture."[11] God's Word is sufficient for the Christian and for the Church. Consequently, there is no need for additional authority and revelation. It is not difficult to appreciate how this cut against the grain of the Catholic Church's two-source theory of authority.

Sola Scriptura, then, is the assertion that Scripture alone is the highest and final authority because it is divinely inspired, inerrant, and sufficient. The underlying issue in the Reformation was that of authority. The Reformers sought to implement Scripture alone as the highest and final authority because they understood tradition, church councils and popes are human, prone to error, and thus insufficient. Consequently, they could not operate at the same level of authority as Scripture. This was the Reformers' thinking, "[b]ecause Scripture is the God-breathed and therefore infallible word of the living God, it carries absolute unique authority – the authority of God himself...If Scripture truly is the word of almighty God, then the issue of final authority is settled."[12]

Sola Scriptura in Scripture

Given the Reformers' high view of Scripture, it is only logical to explore the Bible to see if it teaches all that they claimed.

Life by Every Word (Deuteronomy 8:3)

We begin our exploration of Scripture with the Old Testament book of Deuteronomy. The title "Deuteronomy" is from a Latin mistranslation of 17:18 ("a copy of this law") meaning "Second Law". The Hebrew title is "These are the Words", a more fitting title for the book which contains a collection of speeches, or sermons, delivered by Moses. As the nation of Israel is on the verge of entering the Promised Land, Moses delivers an exposition of the Law. His aim was to convince Israel to trust and obey God. In his second sermon, he recounts the lessons that God taught Israel in the wilderness (8:1–20). As part of this section, he makes it clear that one lesson was dependence on the Word of God alone (v. 3):

> [1] The whole commandment that I command you today you shall be careful to do, that you may live and multiply, and go in and possess the land that the LORD swore to give to your fathers. [2] And you shall remember the whole way that the LORD your God has led you these forty years in the wilderness, that he might humble you, testing you to know

> what was in your heart, whether you would keep his commandments or not. ³ *And he humbled you and let you hunger and fed you with manna, which you did not know, nor did your fathers know, that he might make you know that man does not live by bread alone, but man lives by every word that comes from the mouth of the LORD.* ⁴ Your clothing did not wear out on you and your foot did not swell these forty years. ⁵ Know then in your heart that, as a man disciplines his son, the LORD your God disciplines you. ⁶ So you shall keep the commandments of the LORD your God by walking in his ways and by fearing him.

Moses is seeking to emphasise to a new generation the importance of remembering. The generation of Israelites who had just died in the wilderness did so because they failed to remember God's goodness to them and were justly disciplined. Moses, speaking to the new generation, encourages them to remember all that happened to their forefathers and learn the lessons. As verse two makes clear, these events were to humble the people. God desired that they would experience the difficulties of the wilderness in order that they might fall back on Him.[13] He did not desert them. God provided food (v. 3) and did not permit their clothing to wear out or their feet to swell (v. 4). They were disciplined, humbled, and provided for in the wilderness by God. This new generation are to remember that, and so trust and obey God.

It is only in hearing and learning the history of their people and the Word of God that Israel will determine to trust and obey God. This, they learn as God humbles them. Moses states unequivocally that God did these things so "that he might make you know that man does not live by bread alone, but by every word that comes from the mouth of the LORD" (v. 3). God led Israel into circumstances in which life was solely dependent upon God through His daily provision of manna. This daily bread was more than physical sustenance. It was "the fruit of a daily creative exercise of the Word of God."[14] The lesson Moses was stressing is that the key to life is not the heavenly bread, but the Word of God that provided the bread.

Life is not the physical food one eats, but the nourishment that comes from the mouth of God.[15]

Deuteronomy 8 opens with the promise that obedience to the command of God will bring life (v. 1) and closes with the warning that disobeying the voice of God leads to death (v. 20). This suggests that with the phrase "every word that comes from the mouth of the LORD" (v. 3), Moses is referencing God's written revelation – the Law given at Sinai. This suggestion fits the context of Deuteronomy 8, and indeed, the entire book. There is a clear emphasis on reading the Law throughout. For example, in 17:18–20, the king is commanded to copy out the book of the law and read it all the days of his life. In 31:9–11 Moses himself writes out the law. Giving it to the Levites, he commands them to read it to all Israel every seven years. As two Old Testament scholars put it, "In Deuteronomy the word of God is authoritative and *written*...[Thus] the book reaffirms in Israel the idea of a 'canon,' a collection of *written* materials by which the life of the nation would be administered."[16] Moses is calling the nation of Israel to read, learn, know, and obey this *written* law, for by it comes life.

It seems to me that this is what the Reformers were arguing for: man lives by the Word of God alone. Moses implies in Deuteronomy 8:3 that the Word of God is inspired (it comes from God), inerrant (it requires our trust because it is true), sufficient (it is all we need), and therefore authoritative (it demands our obedience). Life comes by every Word of God. As Deuteronomy makes clear though, this is not some mystical Word of God we are seeking—it is the *written* Word!

Living by Every Word (Matthew 4:1–11)

We turn now to the New Testament. Matthew's Gospel is clearly written with a Jewish audience in mind. As such, it is unsurprising to observe numerous fulfilment themes throughout it. This strong sense of continuity, between the Old Testament and the New Testament, is most likely why Matthew is placed at the beginning of all extant New Testament manuscripts. Just as Moses delivered a number of sermons in Deuteronomy, so Jesus delivers five in Matthew. Each of these sermons end with the statement: "And when Jesus had finished these sayings" (7:28; 11:1; 13:53; 19:1; 26:1).

The passage that we are particularly interested in occurs immediately prior to the first sermon (the Sermon on the Mount, Matt. 5–7). The opening chapters of Matthew detail Jesus' birth, baptism and temptation. In Jesus' temptation, he exemplifies the very reliance on God's Word that Moses called for from Israel. After the assertion of life by every word, we witness Jesus living by every word (Matt. 4:1–11).

We must be careful that we don't force this passage into saying more than it does. It is unlikely that Matthew was thinking about the believer's use of Scripture in general as he records Jesus' temptation. Rather, Matthew is making a Christological statement. He is teaching his readers who Jesus is. To some extent, he is portraying Jesus as a new Adam. In the Garden of Eden, blessed with all the resources he could need, Adam was tested and failed. Jesus, on the other hand, is tested in the wilderness without resources and triumphs.[17] However, a more convincing approach is that Matthew is portraying Jesus as the new Israel (this theme has already appeared in Matthew, most notably 2:13ff.). Just as Israel wandered in the wilderness for 40 years, so Jesus is in the wilderness for 40 days and nights. Moreover, Jesus quotes from Deuteronomy three times in the wilderness (v. 4, cf. Deut. 8:3; v. 7, cf. Deut. 6:16; v. 10, cf. Deut. 6:13). As we noted above, Deuteronomy 8 details Israel's failings in the wilderness, but this is to be contrasted with Jesus' victory in the wilderness.[18]

Tellingly, as Jesus is presented as the new and victorious Israel, it is with the Word of God as his weapon. This fact must not be overlooked. It is surely significant that Jesus rebuffs each and every approach of Satan by quoting Scripture. The obedience to God's Word, called for by Moses in Deuteronomy, is now observed perfectly in Jesus. Don Carson writes: "Israel's hunger had been intended to show them that hearing and obeying the word of God is the most important thing in life …More necessary than bread for Jesus was obedience to God's word."[19] Jesus' attitude to God's Word is clear: it is to be obeyed.

There are also subtle signs about Jesus' understanding of Scripture in Matthew 4. First, the phrase, "it is written", does not simply mean that the words are physically written on a scroll somewhere. Rather, the implication is that Scripture remains reliable throughout the ages. This sermon, preached by Moses more than 1,000 years prior and to a different audience, remains trustworthy and reliable in Jesus' day. Second, there is a comprehensiveness hinted at by the fact that Jesus' quotation of Deuteronomy 8:3 is first. Jesus affirms that the whole of Scripture is beneficial because man lives by every word which comes from the mouth of God. Third, Jesus acknowledges the divine source of Scripture—it comes from God.[20]

We are again observing what the Reformers taught on Scripture, found in the pages of Scripture. Its source is God, its content is reliable, and so, it is to be our final authority. In many ways, Jesus' response to Satan and his temptations was Scripture alone.

Sola Scriptura Today

In closing this chapter, it is necessary to consider in what ways *Sola Scriptura* may be relevant today.

Scripture is Enough

Given the scientific and social advancements since the period in which Scripture was written, it may seem that Scripture does not always speak to the circumstances we find ourselves in. You will not find the terms cigarette, cyberespionage, smartphone, selfie or transgender in it. This has led to Scripture's relevancy in the twenty-first century being questioned—Is Scripture really enough?

Yet to ask this question is to misunderstand the fundamental nature of Scripture and its sufficiency. Scripture is enough, but we must understand the way in which it is enough. Kevin DeYoung helps us on this front:

> To affirm the sufficiency of Scripture is not to suggest that the Bible tells us everything we want to know about everything, but it does tell us everything we need to know about what matters most. Scripture does not give exhaustive information on every subject, but in every subject on which it speaks, it says only what is true. And in its truth we have enough knowledge to turn from sin, find a Saviour, make good decisions, please God, and get to the root of our deepest problems.[21]

We have not been left to our own devices. We are not left to pursue some mysterious word from above. God has spoken. We know His truth. It is easily accessible in His Word. Kevin DeYoung correctly concludes, "The word of God is more than enough for the people of God to live their lives to the glory of God... The question is whether we will open our Bibles and bother to listen."[22] Do not fret about the latest advancements and the absence of their terminology in Scripture; Scripture remains sufficient today.

Scripture and the Church

In affirming that Scripture is enough, we must not miss that community is a great aid in understanding Scripture correctly. While acknowledging that Scripture must reign supreme over all church traditions, Terry Johnson warns that tradition does have a role to play. It is, of course, a subordinate role, but a positive role nonetheless.[23]

It is true that during the Reformation, Luther, Calvin and others fought against holding tradition too highly as an authority. However, it is often overlooked that they also fought against holding tradition too lowly as an authority. In the sixteenth century there was a radical wing to the Reformation who upheld *Solo*, or *Nuda*, *Scriptura* (only Scripture). They argued that "every individual has the unfettered right to interpret Scripture in whatever manner seemed right to him or her."[24] This undoubtedly sounds vaguely familiar to the twenty-first century reader. Today is an age in which many pay little attention to the longstanding doctrines of the Church. Rather, every individual has become their own final authority on the meaning of Scripture.

It is imperative to remember that the Reformers argued that Scripture was to be interpreted in and by the Church. It is pure arrogance to ignore how the Church throughout history has interpreted the Scriptures. In fact, by reading this book you are engaged in the very activity of exploring how the Church have interpreted Scripture. Historic interpretations, Christian creeds, and the tradition of the Church are all of benefit to us, even if they are not binding.

What we are saying is that the Church has a role to play alongside Scripture. Pastors, elders, and the covenant community help us to understand what Scripture teaches. *Sola Scriptura* does not permit rampant individualism. Scripture is our final authority, but we discern its meaning as a community.

Delighting in Scripture

Finally, here are three practical things we can do today which will help us to delight in God's precious gift of His Word.

First, study Scripture. If the Bible is the divinely inspired, totally inerrant, and ultimate authoritative Word of God then Christians should devote much energy to knowing and understanding it. This is not always easy. It takes time, diligence, and intelligence. But by God's grace we are capable of these things. As we begin to appreciate the power and beauty of Scripture, we delight in it.

Second, obey Scripture. We must put into practice that which we know and understand. The Principal of the Irish Baptist College, in Moira, Northern Ireland, has written: "Of course, the whole idea of subscribing to the authority of Scripture is meaningless unless we are prepared to bring our whole lives under its authority."[25] We cannot pick and choose which elements, or parts, of Scripture we will obey. Given its source, nature, and content we must submit our whole lives to it. But when life is lived in accordance with God's Word, delight is the effect.

Third, share Scripture. There is no better gift we can give to our brothers and sisters in Christ than the Word of Christ (Col. 3:16). Likewise, there is no better gift we can give to the world around us than the Word of Christ. Just as we observed with Calvin's ministry in Geneva, so it is possible that as the Word of God is faithfully proclaimed, we, too, will see transformation. Witnessing this brings delight.

Conclusion: Our Confidence

It seems to me that one of the most pressing needs of the Church in the twenty-first century is the return to a high view of Scripture. It has sadly been maligned across Christianity at large, and, surprisingly, even within evangelical circles. We must find once more an attitude before Scripture which encourages reverence, acceptance and adherence to both its authority and message.[26]

The Reformation reminds us that "the lesson of history is the unique power of the Bible to regenerate lost sinners, transform their lives, and build churches."[27] The power and beauty of God's Word remains because its source, nature, and authority remain the same. It is the Church's trust which has waned. Instead, may we be a people who boldly proclaim: "Our confidence is this: our Bible is the very Word of God."[28]

2

SOLA GRATIA
Grace Alone

Erasmus: Hero or Villain?[1]

The underlying issue in the Reformation was that of authority. Did the Church's final authority reside in the Papacy or in the Scriptures. The Reformers clearly argued that Scripture was the final authority, hence the development of the Reformation doctrine of *Sola Scriptura*. With that in mind, it is fitting that we begin this chapter by introducing a man named Desiderius Erasmus.

Erasmus was born between 1466 and 1469 in Rotterdam, Netherlands. As a child he was educated in Deventer, in a School run by the Brethren of the Common Life. Good education was high on this community's agenda. Erasmus, being a bright student, found himself well educated. After a brief period as a monk, he was afforded the opportunity for further learning by studying in Paris, Oxford, and Turin. It is not difficult to understand why he emerged as one of the preeminent humanist scholars of his day.

During Erasmus' time in England, the seeds were sown for what has been termed Erasmus' "greatest work". While in Oxford, he became aware of a few issues with the text of the Latin Vulgate Bible, that used by the Catholic Church, when compared to the original Greek. This stirred him to put his superior education and intellect to use in the service of religion and Scripture. Erasmus published his critical text of the Greek New Testament in 1516. Unsurprisingly, this was to be of considerable aid to the Reformers in their knowledge, understanding, and consequently, teaching of the Scriptures.

It has, therefore, been suggested that Erasmus laid the egg that Luther then hatched. Although Protestants are prone to mark the beginning of the Reformation with Martin Luther nailing his *95 Theses* to the church door in Wittenberg, there are a number of factors that led to this point. One such factor was Erasmus' gift of his Greek New Testament. Luther himself acknowledged the role that Erasmus played in the trajectory of the Reformation. Using the imagery of Moses failing to enter the Promised Land, Luther argued that Erasmus had shown the world the evil of the Roman system, but was not able to show the good and lead on into the land of promise. Erasmus had laid the egg, but he was unable to hatch it.

This positive influence that Erasmus had on the Reformation is important to note, because instead of progressing to become one of the heroes in the story of the Reformation, Erasmus is soon branded a villain. His humanist leanings led Erasmus to think too highly of the ability of humanity. Subsequently, it is against Erasmus' writings on free will that the Reformation doctrine of *Sola Gratia* developed. The debate concerning *Sola Gratia* revolves around humanity's contribution to their salvation. Erasmus, among others, suggested that there was some capacity within individuals to seek out and earn merit with God. The Reformers, however, argued that humanity had no capacity within themselves to desire, or earn, salvation. Rather, from beginning to end, they argued that salvation is a work of God. Salvation is *Sola Gratia*; by grace alone.

An Age-Old Battle

This battle, over humanity's capacity to desire and contribute to salvation, is one that has raged for centuries. It could be understood to have originated with Jesus' skirmishes with the Pharisees. Alternatively, it could have originated with Paul's confrontation of the Judaisers. Both the Pharisees and the Judaisers were keen to give some credit to humanity in their ability to seek God, or to present themselves acceptable in some way to God. Jesus and Paul, however, made it clear that humanity, in their fallen state, is in no way acceptable to God.

An Age-Old Battle: Augustine and Pelagius

These battle lines were famously drawn in the fourth century. A British monk named Pelagius took aim at the North African Augustine and his grace-filled theology. Michael Horton summarises Pelagius' complaint in this way:

> Pelagius and his supporters concluded that the power of sin and divine judgement for it had their cause in individual choice rather than inborn sinfulness. Human beings become sinners by following Adam's poor example, and they become holy by following Christ's good example.[2]

This was not how Augustine understood Scripture. Rather, as Augustine read Scripture, he observed that "God must first make himself known to us and call us before we can call upon him. This highlights the priority of God's grace in salvation."[3]

The lines are clear. Pelagius essentially argued that humanity has it within themselves to desire and earn salvation. Augustine made it clear that there would be no salvation without God's gracious initial movement toward humanity. Despite this battle, the medieval church did not reject the doctrine of grace. Rather, it was their misinformed understanding of grace, and the consequent pastoral misuse, that brought it to the fore again during the Reformation.

An Age-Old Battle: Luther and Erasmus

This very same battle drove a wedge between Martin Luther and Desiderius Erasmus. We have already noted Erasmus' positive influence on the Reformation, with the publication of his Greek New Testament. Indeed, Luther and Erasmus exchanged many letters, often commending and advising one another. From 1524, however, there was an irreparable separation over the issue of free will and God's grace. Erasmus favoured Pelagius' view. Luther, however,

> believing that any kind of effort or contribution man may attempt to make toward his own salvation is works-righteousness, and therefore under condemnation, preferred the thorough-going exegesis of Augustine, who magnifies the grace of God.[4]

Erasmus defined free will as "a power of the human will by which man may apply himself to those things that lead to eternal salvation, or turn away from the same."[5] Unsurprisingly, then, Erasmus took issue with Luther's understanding of sin's impact on the human will. Erasmus believed there was something within humanity that could lead them to salvation. He argued that we are capable of making a choice to adhere to the Christian faith. Luther, on the other hand, affirmed "man's total inability to save himself, and the sovereignty of Divine grace in his salvation."[6] At the heart of Luther's understanding of grace was the acknowledgement that grace is something which ultimately comes, not from within, but from without.[7]

Luther's most persuasively argued presentation of *Sola Gratia* is *The Bondage of the Will*. This is a book-length response to Erasmus' arguments in favour of free will. It is a remarkable piece of work; despite being long, dense, and understandably antiquated, it deserves to be read. It has even been claimed that it is "the greatest piece of theological writing that ever came from Luther's pen."[8] In fact, Luther himself considered *The Bondage of the Will* as one of only two pieces of work from his hand that he wanted preserved.[9] This assessment is justified given Luther's theology of justification by grace alone, as set out in *The Bondage of the Will*, became the touchstone for Reformation preaching. Reformer after Reformer, in light of their study of Scripture, found themselves aligned with Luther's position: William Tyndale, Thomas Cranmer, Nicholas Ridley, Hugh Latimer, John Bradford, John Hooper, John Knox, Ulrich Zwingli, Martin Bucer, and Heinrich Bullinger and many others.

Clarifying the Battle Lines

If we are going to explore Scripture, on the topic of *Sola Gratia*, we need to clarify the battle lines. The differences are subtle, but the implications of these differences are significant.

To be fair, neither Pelagius nor Erasmus denied the presence of sin in mankind. Even so, they effectively denied original sin. Earlier, we noted that Pelagius understood individuals to become sinners by following Adam's poor example. The Pelagian, then, would argue that "people are not helpless sinners who need to be redeemed, but *wayward* sinners who need a demonstration of selflessness so moving that they will be excited to stop being selfish."[10] It is important not to overlook the subtle use of the term "wayward" as opposed to "helpless". The fallout, from this change in terminology, is that salvation becomes a choice. This theological outlook on salvation is persistent and pervasive. Charles Finney writes in his systematic theology:

> [R]egeneration consists in the sinner changing his ultimate choice, intention, preference; or in changing from selfishness to love or benevolence; or, in other words, in turning from the supreme choice of self-gratification, to the supreme love of God and the equal love of his neighbour. Of course the subject of regeneration must be an agent in the work.[11]

In short, Finney is arguing that humanity is entirely capable of being an agent in the work of salvation from within themselves.

This is the Pelagian battle line. For those who aligned themselves with this approach, and Rome became among them, justification became a process in which a bad person made themselves better.

Luther, in drawing the battle line for *Sola Gratia*, could not be clearer. Humanity makes no positive contribution to their salvation. Sinful humanity is certainly wayward, but they are also entirely helpless. Due to their sin, they are incapable of choosing God. Luther is unambiguous: humanity has no claim upon God because God owes them nothing but just judgement for their sin. Edwin Ewart summarises it in the following way:

> It is clear then, grace is vital to any theology that purports to be biblical and the Reformers in their day were gripped by this fact. In particular, they were convinced that Scripture ruled out any idea that fallen human beings can somehow co-operate with God's grace and make a contribution to their salvation. Rather, for the Reformers, "salvation begins and ends with God's gracious initiatives in Christ".[12]

In short, from beginning to end, salvation is *Sola Gratia.* It is by grace alone, initiated by God alone. This was the Augustinian battle line which lived on in Reformation theology. For those who aligned themselves with this approach, it was explicitly clear that justification was a forensic pronouncement based on the imputed righteousness of Jesus Christ.

Sola Gratia in Scripture

Sheer Grace in the Face of the Nations (Deuteronomy 7:7)

We begin our brief foray in Scripture by returning to Deuteronomy, a collection of speeches or sermons delivered by Moses on the edge of the Promised Land. In the area of Moab, as Israel is on the brink of entering this land flowing with all good things, Moses delivers an exposition of the Law. His aim was to convince Israel to trust and obey God. In his second sermon (which began at 4:44), Moses elaborates on why Israel is a holy nation to God:

> ⁶ For you are a people holy to the Lord your God. The Lord your God has chosen you to be a people for his treasured possession, out of all the peoples who are on the face of the earth. ⁷ *It was not because you were more in number than any other people that the Lord set his love on you and chose you, for you were the fewest of all peoples,* ⁸ but it is because the Lord loves you and is keeping the oath that he swore to your fathers, that the Lord has brought you out with a mighty hand and redeemed you from the house of slavery, from the hand of Pharaoh king of Egypt. ⁹ Know therefore that the Lord your God is God, the faithful God who keeps covenant and steadfast love with those who love him and keep his commandments, to a thousand generations, ¹⁰ and repays to their face those who hate him, by destroying them. He will not be slack with one who hates him. He will repay him to his face. ¹¹ You shall therefore be careful to do the commandment and the statutes and the rules that I command you today. (7:6–11)

The beginning of Deuteronomy 7 makes it clear that all that is said in this chapter is in the context of clearing the Promised Land of its current inhabitants (see vv. 1–5). Moses' charge to the people is that everything in this land that has been consecrated to idols must now be consecrated to the wrath of the One True Living God. The Israelites are to embark on a holy war. Yet we must not be sidetracked by this mention of holy war, as the focus of this chapter is on Israel's status as the people of God.

The reality of Israel as God's chosen people stands at the centre of this chapter; indeed, the whole chapter revolves around this truth.[13] It is in this light that we must grapple with the elimination of the current inhabitants of the Promised Land. The charge to eliminate them is really a test of Israel's love for God. More, it is only in the consecrated destruction of those now living in the Promised Land that the goal of Israel's holiness will be achieved.[14] This suggestion fits the theology of Deuteronomy as a whole:

> Yahweh's election of Israel to be his covenant people receives special attention...Moses emphasizes that Yahweh's election had nothing to do

with physical or spiritual superiority (7:6–8; 9:1–23), but was an act of sheer grace, grounded in his love for the ancestors (4:32–38) and their descendants (7:6–8). In so doing the book of Deuteronomy presents the nation of Israel as an incredibly privileged people.[15]

Deuteronomy 7:7 is a perfect example of this.

In the preceding verse, Israel is identified as a privileged people; they are a holy, chosen, and consequently treasured possession. These privileges are based on their relationship to God, a relationship that is denoted by the use of the relational term for "people".[16] The English phrase, "treasured possession", translates a single Hebrew word that speaks of great value. On only eight occasions is this Hebrew word used in the Old Testament: six times it refers to Israel and twice to the great treasure of kings.[17] This is the privilege that the people of Israel enjoy in relationship with the Creator God, known to them as Yahweh. However, knowledge of this privilege poses a danger. There is, surely, a temptation to boast in this privilege, thus Moses reminds Israel that it is through God's sheer grace alone.

Deuteronomy 7:7 makes it explicitly clear that it is God's sovereign love, faithfulness, and grace, and only this, that explains Israel's election. It was not that a holy character, already present in Israel, indicated their inherit merit. It was not that numerical superiority encouraged the privilege of election. Rather, it was the result of divine choice. God had chosen Israel. Indeed, verses 7 and 8 are bursting with grace: they burst with God's affectionate grace as God sets His love on this people (v. 7a); they burst with God's electing grace as God chooses this people (v. 7b); they burst with God's steadfast grace as God's reminds them that He keeps His promises (v. 8a); and they burst with God's redeeming grace as God reminds the people that it was He who delivered them from slavery in Egypt (v. 8b). Interestingly, this is the first use of the term "redeem" in the book of Deuteronomy.[18] Martin Luther summarises it nicely: "[God] comes and takes away all glory and confidence in their works."[19] This is nothing but the work of God, *Sola Gratia*.

Moses appears to ponder the question, "Why does God love Israel?" in Deuteronomy 7:6–8. While he does not explicitly answer the question, his suggestion appears to be that God loves Israel simply because God loves Israel. There is nothing in Israel that compels God's love. As Johann Peter Lange writes: "Such a pre-eminence has its ground not in anything external…[it] was merely the fulfilment of the promise of God to the fathers, a promise according to grace, not implying any merit or pre-eminence on the part of the people."[20] The source of the privileged covenant relationship that Israel enjoys with God lies in God alone. It is an act of loving-kindness, initiated by love, and exemplifying sheer grace. It is *Sola Gratia*. Israel had no claim upon God; it was God's sovereign love, faithfulness, and grace, and only this, that explains Israel's election.

Is this not what we have observed the Reformers arguing for? Salvation (a privileged covenantal relationship with the Creator God) is *Sola Gratia*, and therefore humanity has no claim upon Him. Moses is asserting precisely this in Deuteronomy 7. He tells Israel they are a holy people, chosen by God, and thus a treasured possession. There is no other reason for all of this than that God simply chose them. Terry Johnson is correct:

> One can plunge no deeper than Deuteronomy 7:7 – He loves us because He loves us. Nothing we have done, nothing he might have seen or foreseen has attracted, earned, or merited his favour. Our salvation is of God's sheer mercy and grace alone.[21]

Sheer Grace in the Face of all Powers (Ephesians 2:1–10)

In considering grace alone, it is perhaps unsurprising that we turn to one of the most oft quoted passages of Paul, Ephesians 2:1–10. It is good that this passage is familiar to most, but this familiarity must not breed contempt.

When Paul was writing this letter, Ephesus was a significant city. It boasted a population in excess of 250,000, spread across a thriving city-centre and a network of outlying villages (or as we would term them, suburbs). If Ephesus, as a city, was to be given a theme it would have been power. As a port city, it was a powerful commercial centre with both goods and capital exchanged in the harbour area. As a sophisticated city, it was home to a powerful government who ruled effectively (see Acts 19). The architecture of the city was impressive: there was a theatre that held up to 20,000 people, and it boasted an imposing sporting stadium in which games were regularly held. All of this reinforced the desire for, and enjoyment of, power. In addition to all of this, Ephesus was also home to the temple of Artemis/Diana, a goddess of power in a variety of spheres of ancient life. The city was consumed with the concept of power. This makes what Paul wrote in Ephesians 2:1–10 all the more compelling.

Ephesians 2 opens with a devasting description of humanity's condition apart from God:

> [1] And you were dead in your trespasses and sins [2] in which you once walked, following the course of this world, following the prince of the power of the air, the spirit that is now at work in the sons of disobedience.

In short, outside of relationship with God, Paul's readers in this powerful city were dead. The term that Paul uses refers to a corpse, whether an animal or a human. It describes something that no longer possesses the vital ingredients of life.[22] Paul's readers, due to trespasses and sins, were at one time as unresponsive as a corpse. Worse still, in addition to being unresponsive, they were also under the control of the power of another. Their thoughts and actions were directed by hostile powers. This is not simply a tirade against the Ephesians though; we all once lived in this manner (v. 3). Jew or Gentile, male or female, rich or poor, powerful or weak: at one point everyone was dead in sin, at the beck and call of hostile powers.

Indeed, many still are. These words cut against the grain in Ephesus, because they make it abundantly clear that humanity is utterly helpless. Humanity is powerless in the face of their own sin.

The next two words change everything, except the powerlessness of humanity: "But God" (v. 4). They simply reinforce human powerlessness. Yet, from these words on, "Paul zeroes in on the transformation God accomplished in bringing those who were spiritually dead into new life in Christ."[23] In his action, God makes the Ephesian believers alive (v. 5), gives them positions of honour and authority (v. 6) and through that gives power to the believer. It is imperative, however, that we recognise that this is an act of God alone. It is sheer grace. Just as in Deuteronomy, the motivation is solely God's grace, not anything in humanity:

> [8] For by grace you have been saved through faith. And this is not your own doing; it is the gift of God, [9] not a result of works, so that no one may boast.

The commentators are virtually in unanimous agreement on this point. John Stott writes:

> Indeed the major emphasis of this whole paragraph is what prompted God to act on our behalf was not something in us (some supposed merit) but something in himself (his own unmerited favour)...only "grace" could rescue us from our deserts, for grace is undeserved favour.[24]

Likewise, Peter O'Brien writes:

> God's magnificent rescue from death, wrath, and bondage is all of grace. It neither originates in nor is effected by the readers. Instead, it is Gods own gift, a point which Paul goes out of his way to emphasize by changing the normal word order and contrasting "God's" with "yours".[25]

In this last sentence, O'Brien is referring to the Greek word order at the end of verse 8. A very wooden translation of the final clause in verse 8 could read: "this not from you, God is the gift." "You" is contrasted immediately with "God", and this is reflective of the passage as a whole.

> Klyne Snodgrass summarises it like this:
>
>> Grace is the key ingredient and by necessity comes first; everything else flows from and builds on a theology of grace. Grace means the completely undeserved, loving commitment of God to us. For some reason unknown to us, but which is rooted in his nature, God gives himself to us, attaches himself to us, and acts to rescue us. Though wrath should have come, saving grace comes instead. This action is rooted in God's very nature. The initiative always lies only and completely with him. No human action could remove us from the plight in which we are found.[26]

This message, *Sola Gratia*, would have challenged the prevailing culture in a city consumed with the concept of power as Ephesus was. Here, Paul is telling the Ephesian Church that they were powerless in sin and powerless to save themselves from it. But, God acted, and the result of this sheer grace is an incredible salvation wrought by grace alone. Instead of seeking power, the believers living in Ephesus should now acknowledge their humility. John Stott suggests "[w]e will not be able to strut round heaven like peacocks. Heaven will be filled with the exploits of Christ and the praises of God."[27] Surely he is correct, for this is the reality of *Sola Gratia*. The Reformers were right to argue that we can do nothing to save ourselves, because this is exactly what Paul is stating in Ephesians 2. The testimony of Scripture supports Augustine's position.

Sola Gratia Today[28]

Our Theology of Salvation

The doctrine of *Sola Gratia* remains relevant today, because it has something to say to the most basic human question: "What must I do to be saved?" Writing shortly before his death in 2000, James Montgomery Boice offered this analysis of modern Christianity:

> Today, large numbers of evangelicals undermine and effectively destroy this doctrine by supposing that human beings are basically good; that God owes everyone a chance to be saved; and that, if we are saved, in the final analysis it is because of our own good decision to receive the Jesus who is offered to us.[29]

Sadly, this analysis remains accurate today. Humbly, but firmly, I want to make it clear that this line of argument, that Boice has correctly identified as prevalent, makes a mockery of God. This line of argument makes God and His salvation plan a mere pawn in the bettering of our own lives. This line of argument makes Jesus' call to repentance a cheap insurance policy that we can either take or leave. In short, this line of argument makes us more powerful than God—we choose whether he saves us or not. While Christians are unlikely to ever express it in this manner, it is how many professing Christians essentially function.

The Reformers, however, had no such thoughts about the eternal God. Rather, they argued that, at its root, grace is the determination of God to look upon sinful humanity with favour and deliver us from our just desserts. More, it was while we were still sinners that God acted to save us (Rom. 5:8). *Sola Gratia* reinforces that our salvation has nothing to do with our goodness, our ability, or even our intentions. On the other hand, it has everything to do with God's might and power to rescue helpless humanity. Terry Johnson explains, "[a]n accurate assessment of human depravity is vital if the graciousness of the gospel is to be understood and experienced."[30] We are utterly helpless and need someone to save us.

At a time when our theology of salvation is so often up-side-down and in-side-out, *Sola Gratia* offers a timely corrective. Edwin Ewart writes:

> [T]he conviction that the grace of God alone is what saves the sinner rules out all forms of self-salvation whether in terms of contribution or co-operation. Instead, the gospel confronts us with our complete

> inability and the realisation that apart from the grace of God we stand condemned in the sight of a holy God.[31]

This grace originates in God, is won by God, and must then be given by God and God alone. In light of *Sola Gratia* our theology of salvation must be ruthlessly God-orientated.

Our Preaching of the Gospel

Our preaching of the gospel must also be impacted by *Sola Gratia*. It is not only our theology of salvation which should be totally God-orientated, but also our proclamation of this message. This is, of course, not only applicable to the content of our preaching (which has been touched upon above), but to our methodology in proclaiming the gospel.

Part of the glory of *Sola Gratia* is that communicating this truth does not rely on our eloquence, reasoning abilities, or attractive and engaging presentations. Rather, it relies solely on the power and grace of God. This is Paul's argument in 1 Corinthians 1–2, as he explains to the Corinthians the apparent "foolishness" of the cross. At the beginning of Romans, he makes the point explicitly: the gospel is the power of God for salvation (Rom. 1:16). Martin Luther, following in Paul's footsteps, declared:

> I will preach it, teach it, write it, but I will constrain no man by force, for faith must come freely without compulsion. Take myself as an example. I opposed indulgences and all the papists, but never with force. I simply taught, preached, and wrote God's Word; otherwise I did nothing. And while I slept [cf. Mark 4:26–29], or drank Wittenberg beer with my friends Philip and Amsdorf, the Word so greatly weakened the papacy that no prince or emperor ever inflicted such losses upon it. I did nothing; the Word did everything.[32]

What caused the Reformation to be so effective? In Luther's mind, it was not his methodology, intellect, or eloquence – it was the Word of God. It was the message of the gospel. All Luther did was preach it, teach it, and write it (in letters and tracts). Luther did nothing, the Word did everything.

It is vital that we avoid the trap of attempting to supplement the proclamation of God's Word with unnecessary tactics. This is not to say that a well-crafted drama, a stunning soloist, funky videos, or rhetorical genius does not aid the message of *Sola Gratia*. But our confidence must not be in the approach, it must be in the message. Carl Trueman correctly asserts:

> For those who hold to the Reformation understanding of salvation by grace alone, the proclamation of the Word of God is the principal means of grace. It is the thing which God uses to force people to reckon with their sin, to drive them to their knees in repentance and then draw them to the resurrected Christ by faith.[33]

The Reformation cry of *Sola Gratia* remains relevant today as it encourages us to place our confidence in the message rather than the messenger and their box of tricks.

Our Sense of Assurance

Sola Gratia is enduringly relevant to our evangelism, as we have observed, but it is also enduringly relevant to our Christian life beyond conversion. *Sola Gratia*, Edwin Ewart argues, "brings a profound sense of security and answers many doubts and fears."[34] Follow the logic: salvation is initiated by God, therefore it is not incumbent upon us to *do anything* to gain this salvation. More, not only is it initiated, it is also accomplished by God in the sending of the Son to earth and, ultimately, to the cross, and then applied to us by the Spirit. Christ's righteousness is then imputed to us. Our salvation, our right standing before God, is based on Jesus' righteousness alone, not our own. There is nothing we can do before, during, or after our salvation which will make us or keep us saved. Salvation is accomplished and applied by God. It is all of God. It is

Sola Gratia. This should bring assurance and ease doubts, for it does not depend on us. Salvation depends on the eternal, unchanging God. We can sing Blessed Assurance heartily only because of *Sola Gratia*.

Conclusion: Wholly of God?

There is some variation with the order in which *Sola Gratia*, *Sola Fide* and *Solus Christus* appear in treatments of the *Five Solas*. The reason I have chosen the order in this book is because salvation is by grace alone, through faith alone in Christ alone. Grace is the broader, underlying, principle in which faith emerges and the object of that faith is Christ. As Packer and Johnson write:

> Here was the crucial issue: whether God is the author, not merely of justification, but also of faith; whether, in the last analysis, Christianity is a religion of utter reliance on God for salvation and all things necessary to it, or of self-reliance and self-effort. 'Justification by faith only' is a truth that needs interpretation. The principle of sola fide is not rightly understood till it is seen as anchored in the broader principle of sola gratia. What is the source and status of faith? Is it the God-given means whereby the God-given justification is received, or is it a condition of justification which is left to man to fulfil? Is it a part of God's gift of salvation, or is it man's own contribution to salvation? Is our salvation wholly of God, or does it ultimately depend on something that we do for ourselves?[35]

The Reformers' answer to these questions rings out loud and clear, "*Sola Gratia*"! From beginning to end, salvation is by grace alone; it is the sovereign gift of the eternal God to the unworthy and underserving. Initiated by God, accomplished by God and maintained by God (Jude 24–25). This glorious truth must remove all boasting from our hearts.[36] Humanity's salvation has always been, and will continue to be, *Sola Gratia*. Praise be to God for his glorious grace (Eph. 1:6).

3

SOLA FIDE
Faith Alone

An Impeccable Monk, a Troubled Sinner, and the Righteousness of God?[1]

In 1505, a young law student named Martin Luther was caught in a vicious thunderstorm. After nearly being struck by a bolt of lightning, and fearing for his life, Luther cried out "Saint Anne, help me! I will become a monk." He survived the storm, remained true to his word, and, to the great disappointment of his father, gave up pursuing a career in law to enter the monastery. On 17th August, 1505, Martin Luther entered the Augustinian Order in Erfurt, Germany.

Luther's aim in becoming a monk was to save his soul. He attempted to fulfil this aim with great energy and effort, fully devoting himself to the task of life in a monastery. He laboured in prayer, fasting, penance, physical punishment, and hours upon hours of confession. In fact, he so wearied those hearing his confession that, on at least one occasion, he was told, bluntly, to go back to his room until he had actually committed a sin. Writing to a friend, Luther records:

> I was indeed a pious monk and followed the rules of the order more strictly than I can express. If ever a monk could obtain heaven by his monkish works, I should certainly have been entitled to it. Of this all the friars who have known me can testify. If it had continued much

> longer, I should have carried my mortification even to death, by means of my watchings, prayers, reading and other labours.

None of this saved Luther's soul, however. He was yet to experience comfort and peace.

Having failed to find the solace that he longed for, Luther went beyond the tasks of daily life in the monastery. In November 1510 he visited the Holy City, Rome. Here he sought the merits of various saints, viewed alleged relics (such as a twig from the burning bush and one of the coins Judas received for betraying Jesus), visited holy sites, attended masses, and supposedly scaled the steps of Pilate's Palace, on his hands and knees, repeating the Lord's Prayer at each step. None of this brought Luther closer to his goal.

A turning point occurred in April 1511, when Luther was transferred from Erfurt to Wittenberg. This move was pivotal in his quest to save his soul. It was in Wittenberg that Luther came across John von Staupitz. Von Staupitz was an educated theologian, of the same Augustinian Order, who taught at the University of Wittenberg. He advised Luther, still searching for peace, to devote himself to the study of Scripture. This advice led Luther down a road from which he would not return. Luther applied himself to doctoral studies at the University of Wittenberg, eventually taking the post of Chair of Biblical studies. He continued to pay careful attention to the Scriptures; in particular, the books of Psalms, Romans, and Galatians.

As Luther studied, he came to wrestle with a phrase in Romans: "the righteousness of God" (Rom. 1:17; 3:5, 21, 22; 10:3). This wrestling was to lead to his conversion, and the salvation of his soul. Here is how Luther records his own conversion:

> I greatly longed to understand Paul's epistle to the Romans and nothing stood in the way but that one expression, "the righteousness of God", because I took it to mean that justice whereby God is just and deals justly in punishing the unjust. My situation was that, although

an impeccable monk, I stood before God as a sinner troubled in conscience, and I had no confidence that my merit would assuage Him. Therefore, I did not love a just, angry God, but rather hated and murmured against Him. Yet I clung to dear Paul and had a great yearning to know what he meant.

Night and day I pondered until I saw the connection between the righteousness of God and the statement that "the just shall live by faith." Then I grasped that the righteousness of God is that righteousness by which through grace and sheer mercy God justifies us through faith. Thereupon, I felt myself to be reborn and to have gone through open doors into paradise. The whole of Scripture took on a new meaning, and whereas before "the righteousness of God" had filled me with hate, now it became to me inexpressibly sweet in greater love. This passage of Paul became to me a gate to heaven…If you have a true faith that Christ is your Saviour, then at once you have a gracious God, for faith leads you in and opens up God's heart and will, that you should see pure grace and should look upon His fatherly, friendly heart, in which there is no anger nor ungraciousness. He who sees God as angry does not see him rightly but looks only on a curtain, as if a dark cloud had been drawn across his face.

Unmistakeably, Luther came to the conclusion that God justifies sinners by grace alone, through faith alone, in Christ alone. The impeccable monk had remained a troubled sinner until he had fully understood Paul's phrase: "the righteousness of God". Luther had realised that he could not save his own soul, salvation is *Sola Fide*, by faith alone.[2]

Sola Fide: Knowledge, Assent, Trust

A Medieval Rollercoaster

The essence of *Sola Fide* did not appear to be a major issue in the debates and discussions of the early church fathers. Thomas Schreiner gives this summary:

> We have to remember that the matter wasn't debated or disputed by the early fathers…When we examine what the early church fathers wrote we see two themes. Justification is ours by the grace of God through faith, and good works are necessary for salvation. These two themes

capture quite nicely the NT writings themselves. In that respect the early church fathers were faithful interpreters of the NT.[3]

It seems that this debate was a product of the medieval church's theology of justification. The problem was an absence of forensic language, and therefore the concept of imputation. For the medieval church, justification was a goal that one moved towards. As Sinclair Ferguson remarks: "It is not difficult to see what deeply disturbed the Reformers about this teaching. Justification became the goal to which the individual moves, not the foundation on which the whole Christian life is lived."[4] Failing to appreciate the forensic nature of justification in Scripture proved problematic for the medieval church's doctrine of saving faith.

The result, in Roman Catholic thought, was the development of two distinct types of saving faith: explicit and implicit faith.[5] For the Catholic, explicit faith could be exercised by those who had an understanding of Scripture, and thus could trust it in their own right. This is *Sola Fide*. However, the majority of the population of Europe were illiterate in their native language, and so had little hope of reading a Latin Bible. Consequently, the Catholic Church argued that implicit faith could be exercised by those who had little or no knowledge of Scripture. Implicit faith, then, meant the individual trusted the teaching of the church. In this manner "[f]aith for the Roman Catholic was trusting the (Roman Catholic) church as teacher; it was believing all that the church teaches."[6]

The distinction between explicit and implicit faith is subtle, trusting Scripture or trusting the church's teaching of Scripture. This, however, was an erroneous understanding of saving faith.

> Moreover, this fundamental error led to a whole series of subsequent errors. For example, since one could be justified through divinely assisted works, one could also lose one's justification through sin. Then again, what one loses through sin one could gain again through penance. Because grace is a "power", not a declaration, it can increase or

decrease according to one's obedience or disobedience, and especially through the use or neglect of the seven sacraments of the church.[7]

The medieval church had got it wrong. Justification is *Sola Fide*, by faith alone. The Reformers are going to largely speak for themselves in explaining this for us.

Luther's Solace in Sola Fide

Luther's inner turmoil, as a pious monk striving to make himself right with God, is logical in light of the medieval church's teaching on saving faith. Equally, Luther's joy in discovering that justification is by grace alone, through faith alone, in Christ alone, is almost tangible.

Unsurprisingly, Luther was "the most outspoken of any in this volatile but determinative period."[8] He boldly declared,

> When the article of justification has fallen, everything else has fallen... This is the chief article from which all other doctrines have flowed... it alone begets, nourishes, builds, preserves, and defends the church of God; and without it the church of God cannot exist for one hour.[9]

It is perhaps from this statement that Luther has been credited with the assertion that justification by faith "is the article by which the church stands or falls." Whether he said it in so many words, or not, does not matter, for it is certainly what he means.

Luther correctly understood that if sinners are justified by faith alone in Christ alone, then the church of his day was in error. To proclaim "the righteousness of God", as Luther had come to understand it, would lead to the collapse of this priest-operated, church-based, works-driven system of salvation. In its stead would rise a Christ-centred, faith-based Christianity. It is clear that Luther, after all his strivings to make himself right with God, took great solace in *Sola Fide*. He writes: "You will never find true peace until you find it and keep it in this...that Christ takes all your sins upon himself, and bestows all His righteousness upon you."[10]

Calvin's Clarification of Sola Fide

Reformation thinking became more logically and systematically presented through the ministry of John Calvin. He agreed fully with Luther on the importance of the doctrine of *Sola Fide*. For Calvin, it was "the main hinge on which salvation turns."[11] Losing this doctrine, then, would mean that "the glory of Christ is extinguished, religion is abolished, the church destroyed, and the hope of salvation utterly overthrown."[12] It is clear Calvin thought *Sola Fide* important, but what exactly did he understand salvation by faith alone to mean? In the *Institutes of the Christian Religion*, Calvin wrote:

> We confess with Paul that no other faith justifies but faith working through love. But it does not take its power to justify from that working of love. Indeed it justifies in no other way but in that it leads us into fellowship with the righteousness of Christ.[13]

The issue that gave rise to *Sola Gratia* was the motivation of God in saving humanity. The issue that gave rise to *Sola Fide* was how humanity could appropriate that salvation. Calvin asserted, "as long as Christ remains outside of us, and we are separated from him, all that he has done and suffered for the human race remains useless and of no value." How then does humanity benefit from Christ's sacrifice? Calvin clarified the issue with the answer, "we obtain this by faith."[14] Calvin's most explicit statement on *Sola Fide* can be found in his commentary on Galatians and Ephesians, where he writes: "Let it therefore remain settled that this proposition is exclusive, that we are justified in no other way than by faith, or, which comes to the same thing, that we are justified by faith alone."[15]

Continued Significance

Luther and Calvin were not alone in appreciating the significance of the doctrine of justification through faith alone. The English Reformer, Thomas Cranmer, stated that this doctrine is "the strong rock and foundation of Christian religion." So much so, that "whosoever denieth [this doctrine] is not to be counted for a true Christian man...but for an adversary of Christ."[16]

The Reformers took this seriously, and they were followed closely by the Puritans. Thomas Watson echoes Cranmer's sentiment in writing:

> [J]ustification is the very hinge and pillar of Christianity. An error about justification is dangerous, like a defect in a foundation. Justification by Christ is a spring of the water of life. To have poison of corrupt doctrine cast into this spring is damnable.[17]

Watson's words are heavily indebted not only to Cranmer, but to both Luther and Calvin. Even two hundred years after the Reformation, they reveal that *Sola Fide* remained a crucial doctrine. Indeed, its continued significance is evident in the 1689 Baptist Confession of Faith:

> Faith thus receiving and resting on Christ and His righteousness, is alone the instrument of justification; yet it is not alone in the person justified, but is ever accompanied with all other saving graces, and is no dead faith, but worketh by love. (11.2)

Defining Sola Fide

James Montgomery Boice offers us some help in moving toward a definition of *Sola Fide* by explaining that "faith is the channel by which justification comes to us or actually becomes ours."[18] Or, as Sinclair Ferguson puts it, "Faith draws everything from Christ and contributes nothing to him."[19] Even though faith is only a channel and draws everything from Christ, it is still imperative to salvation. Boice elaborates,

> [A]lthough it is only the channel by which we are justified, it is also the only channel. This is what is meant by sola fide ('faith alone'). If faith is merely receiving what God has done for us, then it is by faith alone that we are justified – all other acts or works being excluded by definition.[20]

This is what the Reformers and Puritans argued for. Yet, it is not all they had to say on the matter. They further defined *Sola Fide* by helpfully identifying three aspects of saving faith.

The first aspect of saving faith is knowledge. The Reformers argued that comprehension and understanding was central to saving faith. More specifically, the object of this faith must be known. Saving faith must rest upon knowledge, not ignorance. Calvin explains:

> We do not obtain salvation either because we are prepared to embrace as true whatever the church has prescribed, or because we turn over to it the task of enquiring or knowing. But we do so when we know that God is our merciful Father, because of reconciliation effected through Christ (2 Cor. 5:18, 19), and that Christ has been given to us as righteousness, sanctification and life. By this knowledge, I say, not by submission of our feeling, do we obtain entry into the Kingdom of Heaven.[21]

Implicit faith is not saving faith. Our faith, if it is to be saving faith, must be explicit. *Sola Fide* must include knowledge.

The second aspect of saving faith is assent. This builds on the first aspect because it is not simply enough to have knowledge. It is possible to know but not assent, and so it is necessary to be in agreement with the knowledge held, or to assent to that knowledge. Saving faith requires that knowledge makes it to the will. Calvin is instructive:

> It now remains to pour into the heart itself what the mind has absorbed. For the Word of God is not received by faith if it flits about the top of the brain, but when it takes root in the depth of the heart that it may be an invincible defence to withstand and drive off all the stratagems of temptation.[22]

There must, then, be a volitional, or willing, assent to the knowledge of the gospel to enjoy saving faith.

The third, and final, aspect of saving faith is trust. The threefold movement involves gaining knowledge of the content, assenting to the content, and, finally, trusting the content. This entails yielding oneself to the message and demands of the gospel in light of the hope of the gospel. *Sola Fide* is drawing everything from Christ; it is the way we appropriate the salvation won for humanity by Jesus Christ, and on that account necessitates knowledge, assent, and trust.

Sola Fide in Scripture

Trusting God (Habakkuk 2:4)

After extensively quoting the Reformers, and particularly Calvin, it is necessary to explore Scripture to see if there is evidence for their claims. We begin with the little-known book of Habakkuk, and the well-known phrase, "the righteous shall live by his faith" (2:4). This verse is quoted three times in the New Testament (Rom. 1:17; Gal. 3:11; Heb. 10:37–38). The debate amongst scholars is whether the New Testament authors are faithful to the Old Testament context and meaning of the verse. What exactly does "the righteous shall live by his faith" mean in Habakkuk 2:4?

The book of Habakkuk is unique on two counts. First, apart from the primarily narrative book of Jonah, it is the only prophetic book to omit the phrase "thus says the LORD." Second, rather than the prophet Habakkuk addressing the people on behalf of God, he addresses God on behalf of the people. He is the only prophet to do so in such a sustained way. This exchange between God and Habakkuk takes place on the brink of exile, and produces a remarkable book. Habakkuk questions the LORD, the LORD in His grace answers, and "the result is a book that is a timeless witness to God's purposes in a world dominated by corruption and violence."[23] After Habakkuk's second extended question (1:12–2:1), God responds (2:2–5) and in this response, He declares "the righteous shall live by his faith" (v. 4).

Despite the vast amounts of ink spilt on this issue, verse 4 is somewhat innocuous in the context of Habakkuk, as it simply blends into the flow of the book. Habakkuk's question is essentially, "why would a holy and just God permit the despicable Chaldeans[24] to triumph over His very own people?" This is a perfectly understandable question. Indeed, this short book climbs to a climax as Habakkuk asserts that he will await the LORD's answer (2:1).

The LORD responds with the command to write this down (2:2). He proceeds to explain that the fulfilment of this vision will not arrive quickly (2:3). Then with the word "Behold" (v. 4), he indicates the substance of the vision is about to be communicated.[25] Unmistakeably, God describes the Chaldeans. They are arrogant, boastful and unrighteous. But, for those who are righteous and trust God, He promises life. Palmer Robertson explains that trusting "in God is the way the gift of life must be received. This way contrasts with all arrogance and boastfulness."[26] The message is straight forward, the Jews, who are about to experience exile at the vindictive hands of the Chaldeans, must be found trusting the God of Israel, the LORD.

Some find this straightforward meaning difficult to reconcile with the New Testament quotations of this verse. However, as careful exegesis demonstrates, the essential meaning correlates with the message of Habakkuk 2:4 in the flow of the book. Therefore, even though Paul applies this verse to justification in Romans 1:17, the meaning essentially remains the same: you must be found trusting God. Likewise, the author to the Hebrews exhorts his readers to develop a trust that endures, even in the midst of difficult circumstances, and explains that this trust will lead to eternal life (10:37–38). Palmer Robertson concludes:

> So two diverse authors of the NT quote the same OT Scripture with a different emphasis to make significantly different points. Yet each author remains true to the essence of the OT Scripture as recorded by Habakkuk. Paul stresses that by faith a person is justified, and the writer to the Hebrews stresses that by faith a person who has been justified shall live.[27]

This all amounts to the same thing that the Reformers argued for, *Sola Fide*. The Jews facing exile, the Romans reading Paul, the Hebrews hearing the same words, and those across sixteenth century Europe are all encouraged to be found trusting God.

Trusting God-in-the-Flesh (Romans 3–4)

It is not difficult to appreciate that this Old Testament exhortation is given flesh (literally, as we will see) in the New Testament. The most explicit place that this happens is in Paul's letter to the Romans.

The book of Romans is not Paul's systematic theology. Rather, it is a letter that he wrote to the Church in Rome, and it appears that there were two primary reasons motivating the letter. First, Paul appears to be attempting to ease tension between the Jews and Gentiles within the Church. So, he puts both on an equal footing with regards to sin (1:18–3:20). Second, Paul seems to be attempting to develop a base from which to launch his missionary endeavours to Spain (15:14–33). These reasons would explain why Paul's presentation of the gospel is theologically rich and systematically detailed.

After an introduction (1:1–17) and asserting that no-one (Jew or Gentile) is righteous (1:18–3:20), Paul turns to explain what Jesus has done for the Christians he is writing to. Leon Morris, commenting on Romans 3:21–26, argues it "is possibly the most important single paragraph ever written."[28] Indeed, it has long been considered the heart of Romans. With this paragraph, Paul draws a sharp distinction between the assertion that none are righteous, and the proclamation that God's righteousness has now been manifested. John Stott explains:

> 'But now', Paul suddenly breaks in, God himself has intervened... After the long night the sun has risen, a new day has dawned, and the world is flooded with light...It is a fresh revelation, focusing on Christ and his cross...over against the unrighteousness of some and the self-righteousness of others, Paul sets the righteousness of God. Over against God's wrath resting on evil-doers (1:18; 2:5; 3:5), he sets God's grace to sinners who believe. Over against judgement, he sets justification.[29]

The horizon in Romans has been changed. Rather than bringing a charge against all, Paul sets forth the penalty paid for all who will believe.

It really is a glorious paragraph. Paul tells his readers that God's righteousness has been revealed. The contrast is stark: by works of the law, no-one will be justified in God's sight (3:20), but now, apart from the law, God has revealed His foretold righteousness (v. 21). The question on everyone's lips is, "What is this righteousness?" However, the question should really be, "Who is this righteousness?" For the answer is God-in-the-flesh, Jesus Christ (v. 22). The only way that salvation can be achieved is "by [God's] grace as a gift, through redemption that is in Christ Jesus" (v. 25). This Jesus, God put forward as a "propitiation by his blood" (v. 25). The term "propitiation" is a rich word that possesses a variety of concepts, such as atonement, cover, expiation, and the averting of wrath. Paul, undoubtedly due to the supreme importance of what he is saying, appears to repeat himself in verse 26. But it is accompanied by a vital elaboration for truly understanding the righteousness of God. God remains just, while also justifying the sinner. Commenting on this elaboration, the ESV study Bible notes:

> God has shown himself to be just (utterly holy, so that the penalty demanded by the law is not removed but paid for by Christ) but also

the justifier (the one who provides the means of justification and who declares people to be in right standing with himself) and the Saviour of all those who trust in Jesus. Here is the heart of the Christian faith, for at the cross God's justice and love meet.[30]

Therefore, it can be no overstatement to claim that this is "the great turning point in world history."[31]

All that Paul has stated categorically, he now illustrates with an example—Abraham (4:1–25). According to Leon Morris, Paul's premise is: "If God had acted in grace toward Abraham, if Abraham had been justified by faith, then Paul's point is established... Abraham is critically important."[32] Paul extrapolates the critical importance of Abraham in four movements: Abraham is justified by faith (vv. 1–8), Abraham is an example for Jew and Gentile alike (vv. 9–16), Abraham's faith is of a particular nature (vv. 17–22), and Abraham remains relevant for the Roman Church (vv. 23–25).[33]

First, Paul argues that Abraham was justified by faith. The key to this argument is Genesis 15:6 (quoted in 4:3), which explains that Abraham "believed the LORD, and he counted it to him as righteousness." This makes it clear that Abraham was counted righteous before he was circumcised, which is recorded in Genesis 17. Unlike the worker who deserves his wages (Rom. 4:4), Abraham did nothing to merit righteousness. Yet, it was not just Abraham, but David as well (4:6–8). As Thomas Schreiner correctly states, "The citation of Ps. 32 in verses 7–8 demonstrates that justification involves the forgiveness of sins, not the performance of certain works to obtain a right standing with God."[34] It was not works, it was not circumcision, it was by faith that Abraham was justified.

Second, in his justification, Abraham is an example for both Jew and Gentile. This is reinforced in the chronological order of Abraham's being credited as righteous prior to his circumcision. Mark Dever highlights this: "Paul seizes on the chronological order of these two events as crucial for understanding the Old Testament and salvation."[35] Abraham is an example to the Gentiles because his circumcision was a seal of the righteousness he had by faith (v. 11). He is also an example to the Jews because he was the "first Jew". He is an example to those who are circumcised that circumcision isn't enough: they must walk in the faith (v. 12). Either way, because the promised righteousness is of grace, the promise rests on faith (v. 16).

Third, Paul makes it clear that Abraham's faith is of a particular nature. Against all odds, Abraham trusts God. He lives out Yahweh's statement to Habakkuk. Even though his body told him otherwise, Abraham believed God's word to him, and this was credited to him as righteousness. Leon Morris reminds us, "Abraham's faith was profound and its being counted to him for righteousness has meaning for all subsequent believers."[36] The significance is that righteousness can't be earned or reasoned, it is a gift through faith.

Fourth, Paul explains that Abraham remains relevant for the Roman Church. Paul's words are astonishing here, "But the words 'it was counted to him' were not written for his sake alone, but for ours also." (vv. 23–24). Here is the abiding relevance of Scripture:

> The story of Abraham is not merely a historical curiosity. It is directly relevant to the lives of the Roman readers, for the account of Abraham was written for their sakes, so that they too could become part of the family of Abraham and share the faith of Abraham.[37]

Abraham remains a relevant example of *Sola Fide*. Our righteousness is credited to us by faith alone.

In only 36 verses (3:21–4:25) the term "faith" occurs 19 times. Although the term can be used in various ways in Scripture, throughout Romans 3–4 it refers to a whole-hearted trust in something. John Stott's comments are enlightening:

> [I]t is vital to affirm that there is nothing meritorious about faith, and that, when we say that salvation is "by faith, not by works", we are not substituting one kind of merit ("faith") for another ("works"). Nor is salvation a sort of cooperative enterprise between God and us, in which

he contributes the cross and we contribute faith…The value of faith is not to be found in itself, but entirely and exclusively in its object, namely Jesus Christ and him crucified…Faith is the eye that looks to him, and the hand that receives his free gift, the mouth that drinks the living water. [38]

Essentially, the virtue of faith is that in which it is placed. For the Christian, that is Jesus Christ, his person and work (more on this in the next chapter). Additionally, it is imperative to observe from Abraham that faith is not primarily a feeling. Rather, "Faith is based on God's Word, not on the evidences of our senses."[39] We need look no further than Romans 4:19 for confirmation of that. This, Scripture makes clear, is *Sola Fide*: trusting God, and trusting God-in-the-flesh.

Sola Fide Today

As we conclude by offering some primers on application, we will follow the three aspects of saving faith identified by the Reformers: knowledge (head), assent (heart), and trust (hands).

Head

There is no such thing as implicit faith. Vital to *Sola Fide*, then, is an adequate knowledge of what we are placing our faith in. One of the defining features of humanity, as the pinnacle of creation, is the life of the mind. Our cognitive abilities set us apart. The life of the mind is not simply our cognitive abilities, however. It is the application of these cognitive abilities. It is therefore incumbent upon humanity, but the redeemed in particular, to pay careful attention to the life of the mind.[40] Christians must apply their cognitive abilities to that which is true, honourable, just, pure, lovely, commendable, excellent, and worthy of praise (Phil. 4:8).

In a world, where there is a high value, rightly, placed upon learning, and expanding the mind; where we can undertake learning in a variety of fields and disciplines; high on our agenda must always be learning Scripture. The Christian must devote themselves to reading, memorizing, studying, and understanding Scripture. Our heads must be engaged in our Christianity. It is not enough to believe whatever the church you attend believes. We must be Bereans, who search the Scriptures to see if it is so (see Acts 17:10–15). Fill your head with the gospel of Jesus Christ that assures you that the righteous shall live by faith.

Heart

Head knowledge is not enough, as we noted with the Reformers above. What has entered the head must make its way to the heart. We must assent to, we must come to agreement with, the content that we claim to know. This is a movement of the will (or what in modern parlance is termed the heart).

We must foster a love for what we know to be true about the gospel: God's goodness and grace, Jesus' willingness to be sacrificed in our place, the Spirit's work in calling us to Christ and empowering us to live for God's glory. Perhaps the best way to foster this love for doctrine is to see these truths at work in people's lives. Read biographies, ask fellow Christians for their testimony, study Church history and the weaving tapestry that God is creating through the grace-driven effort of His people. Seeing this "content" in action in people's lives will aid the movement from head to heart.

Hands

These three aspects of saving faith are interconnected. The head must comprehend what we believe. Only then can the heart grow to love what the head knows. The effect of this, however, is that the hands are active —life is lived differently.

This touches on the apparent discrepancy between Paul and James. James, famously declared that faith without works is dead (2:17, 26). How then can justification by grace alone, through faith alone, in Christ alone stand? Works are necessary, at least according to James! The Reformers have been credited with the saying, "we are saved by faith alone, but the faith that saves is never alone." Or, as Sinclair Ferguson puts it, "Saving or justifying faith always expresses itself in good works. Unless professed faith is working faith, it is not saving faith and therefore cannot be true faith."[41] That is to say, faith without works is dead—it is not true faith. *Sola Fide* demands that Christians live a life distinct from the unconverted, and in obedience to the law of Christ.

Conclusion: Vital to Effective Ministry

It is apparent from our application, that *Sola Fide* is all encompassing. Every aspect of the Christian's life is impacted: the life of the mind, the life of the emotions, and the life of action. This is why the Reformation cry of *Sola Fide* is so essential to effective ministry today. Terry Johnson declares:

> No other doctrine so illustrates the sinfulness of man and the futility of his efforts to save himself. No other doctrine so glorifies Christ as the sole ground of our salvation. No other doctrine so establishes the security of the believer in Christ. Hence, no other doctrine is so vital to biblical preaching and effective ministry.[42]

This is not a word to theological students and pastors. It is a word to every Christian, to recognise that we draw everything from Christ by faith alone. It is in that, that our righteousness is found, and in that alone. Over 100 years ago J. Gresham Machen stated the same thing:

The true reason why faith is given such as exclusive place by the New Testament, so far as the attainment of salvation is concerned, over against love and over against everything else in man...is that faith means receiving something, not doing something or even being something. To say, therefore, that our faith saves us means that we do not save ourselves even in the slightest measure, but that God saves us.[43]

4

SOLUS CHRISTUS

Christ Alone

Why the God-man?[1]

Anselm of Canterbury was an Italian who, after living in France, was appointed as the Archbishop of England in 1093. He is responsible for one of the most important pieces of theological writing to emerge from the medieval church, *Cur Deus Homo?* (published in 1098). When translated, this Latin title reads: Why the God-man? In this book Anselm explores the reason for the incarnation. His conclusion is, the cross. He argues the only possible ground for salvation is God becoming man and making atonement for sin. Therefore, the necessity for the God-man.

If, as Anselm argues, sin is for someone "not to render his due to God," then it is an infinite offence against God. An infinite offence against God is inexcusable. Anselm writes, "Nothing is less tolerable in the order of things, than for creature to take away the honour due to the Creator and not repay what he takes away." The enormity of sin is that we, the creature, have stolen the honour of God, the Creator. However, this is not all, we are also incapable of giving it back.

If this was not problematic enough, there is a further problem for humanity. As Anselm reasons, "if it is not fitting for God to do anything unjustly or without due order, it does not belong to his freedom or kindness or will to forgive unpunished the sinner who does not repay to God what he took away." Not only has humanity stolen God's honour, and are incapable of giving it back, but God's holy nature will not permit Him to simply overlook sin. God's character will not allow sin to be let alone, disregarded, or forgiven without being dealt with. This, suggests Anselm, is why the God-man is necessary. Sin can only be truly dealt with by one who is both God and man; for it is man who must give honour back to God, and yet it is only God who can truly deal with sin.

The significance of this piece of theological writing from Anselm is widely acknowledged. Stephen J. Wellum asserts, "Beyond dispute Anselm's *Why God Became Man?* was a key theological work on the atonement in the medieval era."[2] However, Anselm's work was not perfect. Wellum continues:

> Yet, for all Anselm's stress on the incarnation, in failing to locate Christ's work within its biblical, covenantal context, he does not adequately develop Christ's covenantal representation and substitution. Anselm does not explain how Christ's obedient life and death as the incarnate Son is the basis for our salvation and how it becomes ours. By not thinking of Christ's mediatorial work in terms of his obedience as our covenant head, Anselm does not unpack the biblical rationale of how Christ's righteousness becomes ours, how Christ's death fully satisfies God's righteousness, and how we benefit from his work by faith union with him.[3]

In short, Anselm failed to explain how all that Jesus Christ achieved as the God-man becomes the possession of the Christian.

The reason why this was problematic was because others soon suggested ways in how Jesus Christ's obedience and righteousness became ours which were often distorted from biblical truth. The way in which Christ's obedience and righteousness became the Christian's continued to be debated. Even though he lived over two centuries later, a prime example is Thomas Aquinas. He suggested that Christ's obedience and righteousness were conveyed to the Christian by the Church. More particularly, by adherence to the sacraments of the Church. This was to become the position of the medieval church and, later, Rome, which is why the Reformers cried *Solus Christus*.

A Joint Venture?

Man and God

Rome did not deny the necessity of Jesus Christ's death. However, as we observed in our previous chapter, they did argue that the Church had a mediatorial role to play in the application of Jesus Christ's obedience and righteousness to the Christian.

The Church was intimately involved in almost every aspect of life in the sixteenth century. All of the major events of life were covered by sacraments in the Church. As an infant, one was baptised; as a youth, one was confirmed; as an adult, one was married; in death, one received the last rites (otherwise known as extreme unction). In addition to these sacraments, which marked significant life events, the average church goer of the sixteenth century would regularly partake of both confession of sin and the eucharist (Mass). There was a seventh sacrament, Holy Orders, which was reserved for the few who entered the priesthood. The medieval hurch claimed that these sacraments conveyed grace on all who partook of them. From the cradle to the grave, individuals were dependant on the Church as they sought salvation. Jesus Christ may have achieved salvation for His people on the cross, but it was only through the church that this grace may be received. It was a joint venture between man and God.[4]

God and Man

Given the material that we have covered in the previous chapters, it is unsurprising to note that the Reformers took issue with this understanding of how salvation was conveyed. It was in response to this understanding that the cry *Solus Christus* developed. Rather than the joint venture of man and God, the Reformers asserted it was the sole venture of the One who is God and man.

James I. Packer argues that "Luther was the first theologian to give prominence to the thought that the satisfaction to God for sin which, as Anselm had established, Christ rendered on our behalf on the cross, was penal and substitutionary in its nature."[5] This may be something of an overstatement, especially if we include the biblical authors as theologians! Nonetheless, the point is well taken. Martin Luther realised that the Roman Catholic Church was attempting to rob the cross of it power. In his effort to combat this error, Luther laboured to make explicit that Jesus took our punishment on our behalf. He argued that the cross was both penal and substitutionary in nature. In doing so, Luther contended that God was satisfied by this sacrifice. As Luther explains:

> Since all of us, born in sin and God's enemies, have earned nothing but eternal wrath and hell so that everything we are and can do is damned, and there is no help or way of getting out of this predicament...therefore another man had to step into our place, namely Jesus Christ, God and man, and had to render satisfaction and make payment for sin through his suffering and death.[6]

This is *Solus Christus*. We, in our sinful state, cannot save ourselves and so another must pay the price for sin on our behalf. The prominence of this in Luther's thinking, writing, and teaching is summed up in his claim that Christian theology is a theology of the cross.[7] Without Jesus Christ's substitutionary work on our behalf there would be no Christianity.

This sentiment was shared by John Calvin. He reiterates it when he writes, "We see that our whole salvation and all its parts are comprehended in Christ."[8] This is elaborated in one of Calvin's most striking and powerful paragraphs:

> If we seek salvation, we are taught by the very name of Jesus that it is 'of him' (1 Cor. 1:30). If we seek any other gifts of the Spirit, they will be found in his anointing. If we seek strength, it lies in his dominion; if purity, in his conception; if gentleness, it appears in his birth. For by his birth he was made like us in all respects (Heb. 2:17) that he might learn to feel our pain (cf. Heb. 5:2). If we seek redemption, it lies in his passion; if acquittal, in his condemnation; if remission of the curse, in his cross (Gal. 3:13); if satisfaction, in his sacrifice; if purification, in his blood; if reconciliation, in his descent into hell; if mortification of the flesh, in his tomb; if newness of life, in his resurrection; if immortality, in the same; if inheritance of the Heavenly Kingdom, in his entrance into heaven; if protection, if security, if abundant supply of all blessings, in his Kingdom; if untroubled expectation of judgement, in the power given to him to judge. In short, since rich store of every kind of good abounds in him, let us drink our fill from this fountain and no other.[9]

In this paragraph John Calvin is unmistakeably proclaiming *Solus Christus*. Christian theology must be a theology of the cross, for it is only in, and through, the substitutionary work of Jesus on the cross that we are able to enjoy the fullness of salvation. This is exactly what is articulated in such striking and powerful manner by Calvin.

As we have already observed, the Roman Catholic Church of the sixteenth century taught that the blessings of salvation won by Jesus can only be applied through the sacraments. For this reason, Calvin directly challenged this false teaching. Calvin asserted, with his characteristic boldness, "The more detestable is the fabrication of those who, not content with Christ's priesthood, have presumed to sacrifice him anew!"[10] It is the practice of the Mass that Calvin is particularly taking aim at here. He took issue with its teaching that Christ is sacrificed each and every time the bread and wine is consumed. Moreover, he was concerned that many believed that it was only by adhering to this sacrament (in addition to the others) that one could receive the blessing of salvation won by Jesus Christ.

Calvin's concern over the Roman Catholic Church's teaching on the Mass was voiced at an earlier date by the Zurich Reformer, Ulrich Zwingli. He stated, "That Christ sacrificed himself once, is to eternity a certain and valid sacrifice for the sins of all the faithful, wherefrom it follows that the mass is not a sacrifice."[11] This is *Solus Christus*; no person or sacrament can provide humanity with salvation except Jesus Christ. He alone is our substitute; he alone can bear our penalty. As Zwingli explains:

> We know from the Old and New Testaments of God that our only comforter, redeemer, saviour and mediator with God is Jesus Christ, in whom and through whom alone we can obtain grace, help and salvation, and besides from no other being in heaven or on earth.[12]

Satisfaction in the Person and Work of Jesus

The Reformers made it abundantly clear that they saw no mediatorial role for the Church with respect to receiving the blessings of salvation. Rather, it is through Jesus Christ alone, *Solus Christus*, that the believer receives these blessings. We have already noted how John Calvin explained the way in which both the person and work of Jesus Christ convey every spiritual blessing to the believer. In all of this, the Reformers were concerned to defend both the person and work of Jesus Christ.

We must be careful, however, not to read current controversies back into history. Although the Reformers made strong statements about the person and work of Jesus Christ, it is important to note that the Roman Catholic Church did not necessarily oppose all of their assertions. For example, both Rome and the Reformers agreed on Jesus' unique identity as God incarnate. From the period of the early church fathers through to the Reformation, the Church spoke largely with one voice on the issue of the person of Jesus Christ. He was the second person of the Trinity in the flesh. The issue was the sufficiency of Christ's work.[13]

Edwin Ewart summarises the growing rift between Rome and the Reformers:

> It was on this matter of the death of Christ then, that the division between Rome and the Reformers was most marked. While apparently confessing the perfection of Christ's sacrifice, Rome still maintained the various "satisfactions" needed to be made by believers (such as penance) and this compromised both Christ's unique person and work.[14]

Here, Ewart perceptively notes an implication of Rome's view. If Christ's work is not sufficient, then Christ's person is no longer unique. If Christ's work is not sufficient, neither is his person. This is elaborated by Ewart:

> The Reformers, on the other hand, insisted that the death of Christ satisfied all the demands of God's law against us and when appropriated through faith believers receive a new standing in God's sight...This is best illustrated in Reformation opposition to the practice of the mass.[15]

We noted this earlier with John Calvin and Ulrich Zwingli. The Roman Catholic Church understood the believer to be able receive all of the blessings of salvation won by Jesus on the cross through observing the Sacraments, particularly Mass. Every celebration of the Mass was believed to be a fresh sacrifice. In this way, both the work of Christ, which it was argued needed to be repeated, and the person of Christ, in that a human priest offers the application of the blessings of salvation, were under attack. Terry Johnson notes:

> Communion is a supper, said the Reformers, not a sacrifice (1 Cor. 11:20). It is served upon "the table of the Lord", not an altar (1 Cor. 10:21). His sacrifice was once for all and anything that weakens our sense of its finality robs it of its glory.[16]

> The sacrifice of Christ was a propitiating, justice-satisfying, wrath-quenching event. By his death the justice of God was satisfied.[17]

The core of the issue is satisfaction in both the person and work of Jesus Christ. There is no space for human cooperation. There are no other means of appropriating the blessings of salvation. Rather, it is *Solus Christus*.[18]

Solus Christus in Scripture

Solus Christus Foretold

John Armstrong asserts, "At the centre of the whole Scripture [the] Reformers saw a person, namely, one person, the God-man, Christ Jesus."[19] The Old Testament is punctuated by promises, predictions and allusions to the One God would send. It would not do justice to look at only one Old Testament passage, so we will briefly survey four passages to see if they hold out the hope of *Solus Christus*.

We begin with "the first glimmer of the gospel."[20] The opening chapters of Genesis, and Scripture, report that God spoke everything we see (and everything we do not see) into creation. Repeatedly, we are told, this creation is pronounced good (1:10, 12, 18, 21, 25). In one instance, it is pronounced very good (1:31). The pinnacle of creation is humanity, male and female (1:26-2:25). But this all changes with Adam and Eve's disobedience of God's only explicit prohibition (3:1–13). As a result, there is an announcement of judgement and salvation, or, in Derek Kidner's words, the first glimmer of the gospel. They are found in Genesis 3:15:

> I will put enmity between you and the woman,
> > and between your offspring and her offspring;
> He shall bruise your head,
> > and you shall bruise his heel.

This is the climax of God's pronouncement of judgement on the serpent (vv. 14–15), before He turns to pronounce judgement on Eve (v. 16), and finally Adam (vv. 17–19). The serpent is explicitly told of his coming defeat, in which the seed of the woman will crush his head. This pronouncement of judgement and salvation is remarkable. As John Sailhamer notes, "It is a momentous moment in Genesis...[These words] are, after all, God's first statements to the first sinner."[21] This first statement to the first sinner is the promise of victory over sin. There are two important elements to note here, however. First, the woman's seed is presented as one that lies in the future.[22] Second, it is possibly significant that it is the woman's seed and not the man's seed that will win this victory. Could this possibly be a veiled allusion to the virgin birth?[23] In the end, Genesis 3:15 does not answer the question of who this seed would be. But it certainly raises the question.

This initial passage is elaborated in Genesis 12:1–3. This second passage is an important expansion on the first. Genesis 12 begins a new section within the book of Genesis. The movement is from the beginning of creation (chapters 1–11), to the beginning of God's people (chapters 12–50). This new people will come from a man known as Abram at this point, but soon to be known as Abraham. In Genesis 12:1–3 God speaks to Abram:

> Go from your country and your kindred and your father's house to the land that I will show you. And I will make of you a great nation, and I will bless you and make your name great, so that you will be a blessing. I will bless those who bless you, and him who dishonours you I will curse, and in you all the families of the earth shall be blessed.

It is vitally important to appreciate the significance of divine speech at this moment in Genesis. As the book moves from focusing on creation to focusing on the people of God, it is marked by the promise of divine blessing mediated through this new people. This new group is constituted of the descendants of Abram. The hope is that the judgement of Genesis 3 will be reversed by God's blessing through the descendants of Abram, a hope hinted at by the repetition of the verb bless. The promised seed from Genesis 3 will be a descendant of Abram and, in so being, will bring a blessing to the world.

For our third passage we must jump forward to 2 Samuel 7. Here Scripture records Nathan's oracle concerning King David and his descendants, more specifically his heirs. King David was perhaps the descendant of Abram who gave God's people most hope of divine blessing. He was, after all, a man after God's own heart (1 Sam. 13:14). Yet, despite his many admirable characteristics, Scripture's narrative soon makes it clear that David is not *the* descendant that God's people have been hoping for. He is not *the* seed who will crush evil's head. Rather, Nathan explains, David will die and his son Solomon will reign in his place. Under Solomon there will be the blessing of building God's House (2 Sam. 7:13). Yet, there is more. Nathan proceeds to promise to David a descendant who will sit on the Davidic throne forever (v. 13). There is a coming king, from among Abram's descendants, who will reign (therefore vanquishing evil) forever.

This king will not be aloof from his people, but will suffer for them. After early promises about a coming Davidic king (Isa. 7:14; 9:6–7; 11:1–16), the prophet Isaiah explains that he will also suffer. Isaiah 53 is an incredibly sophisticated and powerful poem.[24] It is, however, a widely debated portion of Scripture with scholars disputing the identity of the individual in the poem. The options range from Isaiah himself, to an unknown messianic figure, to the nation of Israel. There are strong arguments on all these fronts, but I believe that the best argument results in a Christological understanding. This fourth so-called "Servant Song" actually begins in 52:13. From the outset, the "Servant" is assigned three adjectives that elsewhere are consistently used, almost exclusively, of God: high, lifted up, and exalted (v. 13). This individual seems to be more than a mere human. Added to this is the clear impression of substitution in 53:4–5:

> Surely he has borne our griefs
> > and carried our sorrows
> yet we esteemed him stricken,
> > smitten by God, and afflicted.
> But he was wounded for our transgressions;
> > he was crushed for our iniquities;
> upon him was the chastisement that brought us peace,
> > and with his stripes we are healed

This "Servant" does not simply suffer, nor even suffer innocently. He suffers for someone else's sin.

These four passages in the Old Testament, among countless others, appear to be foretelling a coming individual who will crush the head of evil, bring blessing to all nations, rule and reign on the Davidic throne forever, and suffer in someone else's stead. For those of us who have the testimony of the New Testament this sounds suspiciously like the description of Jesus Christ contained there. It is to that testimony we now turn.

Solus Christus Forthtold

As the New Testament opens Jesus Christ is presented as the seed, the Abrahamic descendant, the Davidic king, and ultimately the substitutionary servant (Matt. 1:1, 21; 20:28). The New Testament then declares that salvation is found in no-one else but Jesus. The New Testament clearly forthtells *Solus Christus*.

To begin with, *Solus Christus* is boldly proclaimed by the Apostle Peter in Acts 4:12, "And there is salvation in no one else, for there is no other name under heaven given among men by which we must be saved." To fully appreciate this statement, we must consider the context. In Acts 3, Peter and John see a lame beggar healed in the power of Jesus' name. This miracle fills onlookers with awe and wonder (3:10), which in turn gives Peter the opportunity to preach about Jesus Christ (3:12–26). Peter does not miss his opportunity to call the crowd to repentance and salvation (see 3:19). All of this commotion, however, brings Peter and John to the attention of the authorities. Once arrested and in their custody, they are asked to explain themselves (4:1–7). In response, Peter makes the bold proclamation that there is salvation in no other name. John Stott clarifies the magnitude of this statement:

> [The] two negatives (no-one else and no other name) proclaim the positive uniqueness of the name of Jesus. His death and resurrection, his exaltation and authority constitute him the one and only Saviour, since nobody else possesses his qualifications.[25]

Simply put, Peter is proclaiming salvation in Christ alone, *Solus Christus*. In recording the history of the early Church, Luke is careful to include the Apostle Peter boldly proclaiming *Solus Christus*. It would appear that the Reformers were merely echoing the Apostles preaching by declaring that salvation is found in Christ alone.

Second, the Apostle Paul forthtells *Solus Christus*. He does so by defending robustly the gospel. The opening passage in his letter to the Churches of Galatia (1:1–10) is perhaps the most striking example of this. Galatians is probably Paul's most combative letter as he attempts to ensure that his readers are not consumed with the message of false teachers. By the time Paul is writing it appears that at least some people have been enticed by the false teachers, and so Paul expresses his astonishment (1:6). Paul cares deeply for these Churches, thus he is at pains to convince his readers that there is no other gospel (1:7). There is only one gospel; the content of which has been delivered in 1:3–5, "the Lord Jesus Christ, who gave himself for our sins to deliver us from the present evil age, according to the will of our God and Father, to whom be the glory forever and ever." Anyone preaching anything different should be accursed (1:8–9). As Philip Ryken summarises:

> The good news of justification by grace alone, through faith alone, in Christ alone, is the only gospel there is. Anyone who says anything

> different – Paul doesn't care who – deserves to go to hell! There is no other gospel, there has never been any other gospel, and there never will be any other gospel.[26]

This pronouncement by Paul, that anyone preaching anything different should be accursed, is a strong denouncement. The Greek word he uses is *anathema*. This is no slap on the wrist that Paul is invoking; rather, it is eternal judgement. He is calling the Churches to invoke God's wrath and damnation on those who would seek to distort the gospel. Paul argues that there is only one gospel, and that is salvation in, by, and through Jesus Christ alone. If anyone claims anything else, let them be cursed to hell. This is a fierce way of proclaiming *Solus Christus*.

Third, the New Testament witness draws our attention to Jesus' priesthood. The book of Hebrews offers an extended treatment of Jesus' priesthood in the central section, running from 4:14–7:28. After this treatment the author to the Hebrews offers a summary statement: "Now the point in what we are saying is this: we have such a high priest" (8:1). It is apparent that "One of the central themes of Hebrews is that Jesus is the high priest, and hence believers should not attach or entrust themselves to any other high priest."[27] This, it seems to me, is exactly what the Reformers were arguing for. It is exactly what they declared in proclaiming *Solus Christus*. The author to the Hebrews was arguing that there was no need for Judaism to mediate the blessings of salvation won by Jesus Christ. Likewise, the Reformers were arguing that there was no need for the Church to mediate the blessings of salvation won by Jesus Christ. Rather, we have a high priest working on our behalf, mediating the blessing he himself won for us (8:1). Thomas Schreiner writes:

> What is striking here is that the author says the main point in his discourse is that Jesus is a high priest who has sat down at God's right hand. In other words, Jesus is a different kind of high priest from Levitical high priests, for his work as high priest is completed and finished, and hence he has sat down at God's right hand. The Levitical

> high priests, on the other hand, continually stand (10:11), for their work as priests is never completed, which demonstrates the inadequacy and ineffectiveness of their priesthood.[28]

In Hebrews 9:11–14, it is made explicit that this work Jesus has completed and finished is his crucifixion and resurrection. Considering all that Jesus has done, and the way in which he continues to apply it to his people, the author to the Hebrews is urging his readers to not forsake Jesus as your high priest. Rather, we must rest entirely in what Jesus has done and is doing for us. This is *Solus Christus*.

The New Testament presents a clear testimony to the fact that the early Church, apostles, and authors of Scripture held to *Solus Christus*. They proclaimed, argued, and declared that salvation is found in Jesus Christ alone. There is no other name, no other gospel, and no other mediator.

Solus Christus Today

The Reformation cry of *Solus Christus* remains important for us today in at least two ways.

The Gospel's Content

First, the gospel's content must be defined by this Reformation cry. As Luther argued, Christian theology is a theology of the cross. Everything either leads to or flows from the cross. The cross is central to Christianity, and thus to Christianity's gospel.

In a previous era of gospel ministry, it is fair to say that many other aspects of Christian theology were neglected for an almost exclusive focus on the cross. This has created a backlash in modern Christianity. In many ways modern Christianity has recovered many aspects of the gospel which had been neglected: the incarnation,

Jesus' obedient life as example, Jesus' teaching, exaltation, and intercessory/mediatorial work. But to highlight these aspects at the expense of the cross and resurrection would be equally wrong.

This has become particularly apparent in the wake of postmodern theology. For example, the focus on incarnational ministry. The argument claims that since Jesus left heaven to be with his disciples, so we must leave our comfort zone to spend time with others. We must be Jesus to the people and pray they respond positively. This, I would argue, is a fair application of the gospel; but it is not the gospel. James Montgomery Boice offers this sage advice:

> The conviction that there is no possibility of heaven apart from faith in Christ has motivated our evangelistic efforts, it has spawned the great missionary movement...The gospel itself is a message about the exclusivity of Christ. And the gospel must be preached to the ends of the earth, so that people who have never heard of Christ can be saved. That is the Christian mission. It is our mandate from the Lord himself. [29]

Our eyes must always be fixed on the cross. All of our gospel endeavours must either lead to or flow from the cross. The central content of any gospel message must be the cross. If not, the message is missing the content that makes it the gospel.

The Gospel's Commission

Second, the gospel's commission must be driven by this Reformation cry. John MacArthur contends:

> Christmas by itself is no gospel. The life of Christ is no gospel. Even the resurrection is no gospel. The Good News is not just that God became man, nor that God has spoken in Christ to reveal a proper way of life for us, nor even that death, our greatest enemy, has been conquered. The Good News is that sin has been dealt with, that Jesus has suffered its penalty for us as our representative, and that all who believe in him can look forward confidently to heaven.[30]

This is the gospel's commission. In a pluralistic age, when many are content to suggest that Jesus is one among many legitimate ways to eternal life, we are in danger of losing our evangelistic and missional zeal. *Solus Christus* permits no such lethargy in heeding the gospel's commission.

If we accept the Reformation cry of *Solus Christus*, understand Scripture to teach that salvation is found only in and through Jesus Christ, and seek to obey Jesus' command to go and make disciples of all nations, it follows that we must be engaged in personal evangelism and global mission. If there is no other way for people to be saved from sin; if there is no other way for eternal life to be gained; if there is no other way to escape the wrath of God. The only option left is to proclaim salvation in Christ alone.

Thus, not only must our content be focused on the cross, but our commission must be driven by the exclusive message of the cross. John MacArthur concludes, "True Christians have always been compelled by the fact that if people don't hear the gospel, they cannot be saved. And if they are not saved, they will spend eternity in hell under the judgement of God."[31] We are compelled by biblical truth, expressed in the Reformation cry of *Solus Christus*, to go into all the world and proclaim salvation in no other name but Jesus Christ.

Conclusion

We can do no better than close with the words of James Montgomery Boice:

> To proclaim Christ alone is to proclaim him as the Christian's one and only sufficient Prophet, Priest and King. We need no other prophet to reveal God's word or will. We need no other priests to mediate God's salvation and blessing. We need no other kings to control the thinking and lives of believers. Jesus is everything to us and for us in the gospel.[32]

5

SOLI DEO GLORIA

Glory to God Alone

Purpose-Driven Death[1]

In 1527, a 24-year-old Scotsman named Patrick Hamilton returned to Scotland. Hamilton had been studying in Germany and was returning as a convert of Martin Luther's gospel. Scotland, however, remained under Catholic influence. Protestants were facing persecution at the hands of King James V of Scotland and Hamilton knew that the same persecution likely awaited him, but he was compelled to preach the gospel to his fellow countrymen. He survived only a matter of weeks proclaiming the very same gospel he had responded to in Europe. On the 29th February 1528, Patrick Hamilton was burned at the stake at St Andrews. This young man gave up his life for the gospel; he gave up his life for the four *Solas* we have already considered. Why? The answer is surely our fifth sola: *Soli Deo Gloria*. Patrick Hamilton's was a purpose-driven death, a death for the glory of God alone.

Almost two decades later a gentleman named George Wishart was also burned at the stake at St Andrews. By all accounts George Wishart was modest, calm, and extremely generous. He gave away most of what he owned to those less fortunate; gladly sharing money, possessions, and often skipping meals to provide for others.

Despite being a university lecturer in Cambridge, after hearing of the hardships that Christians were enduring in Scotland, he soon returned to his homeland.

In addition to Wishart's kindness and generosity the people of Scotland needed a Bible teacher. Wishart duly obliged and began teaching and preaching. The persecutors soon turned their attention to this new Bible teacher. Initially the protests were mild enough, taking the form of heckling during sermons and lectures. Things took a more sinister turn, however, when a priest attempted to stab Wishart as he descended from the pulpit. Wishart's friends quickly understood that the priest had attempted to take Wishart's life, and so sought to teach the priest a lesson by taking his. Wishart spared the priest's life by taking hold of him and declaring: "Whatever you try to do to him will be done to me."

Despite this act of kindness, Wishart found himself following in his Saviour's footsteps by enduring a show trial whereby, like Christ, he was falsely charged, lied about by false witnesses, and ultimately ignored by the judge. Consequently, Wishart was found guilty and sentenced to death. Those present at the so-called trial dragged Wishart outside, tied him to a stake, tied bags of gunpowder to him, and set him alight. It was the 28th February 1546.

As the fire burned brighter and hotter his prayer could be heard amidst the crackling flames: "Saviour of the world, have mercy on me. Father I give my spirit into your hands. I ask God that you forgive these ignorant people who have wrongly condemned me with their lies. I forgive them and I ask that Jesus forgive them." This remarkable prayer was answered as one of the guilty parties fell to his knees and asked for forgiveness. George Wishart gave up his life for the gospel, resolutely enduring hardships and facing death. Why? The answer is surely *Soli Deo Gloria*. Wishart's was a purpose-driven death, a death for the glory of God alone.

These two Scotsmen were willing to surrender their lives for the gospel. Their purpose-driven deaths were based on the conviction that glory must go to God alone, no matter the cost. Terry Johnson asserts: "The Reformers lived and died for Scripture alone, Christ alone, faith alone, and grace alone because they saw that these principles gave all the glory to God and none to man."[2] Indeed, the conviction of *Soli Deo Gloria* is exemplified by John Calvin's demand that he be buried in an unmarked grave to avoid people being enticed to create a shrine in his remembrance.

Reform in Every Sphere

James Montgomery Boice is correct in arguing that "a grasp of the first four *solas* leads naturally to *soli Deo Gloria*."[3] Indeed, we could go further than this and argue that the Reformation cry of *Soli Deo Gloria* is actually central to the Five Solas. The very thing at stake in discussions of Scripture's authority, God's grace, the role of faith, and the unique person and work of Jesus Christ is in fact the glory of God.[4]

It is clearly observable that in the sixteenth century, the glory of God constituted a vital, if not controlling, place in the thinking of the Reformers.[5] That being said, the reality is there has been little-to-no historical debate on this issue. All Christians and Churches of all creeds have consistently acknowledged that God demands and deserves all the glory. Moreover, they claim that the intention in their actions is for that end. The distinction with the Reformers, however, was the claim that *Soli Deo Gloria* demanded reform in every sphere. As Terry Johnson notes: "Theological reform was necessary because the gospel had been muddied by medieval intentions...But reform, then and now, cannot stop merely with theology."[6] The Reformation cry *Soli Deo Gloria* captures the Reformers' belief that the glory of God demands reform in every sphere of life.

Corporate Worship

The first sphere of life to be reformed by the principle of *Soli Deo Gloria* was, perhaps unsurprisingly, corporate worship. Martin Luther revised the liturgy for Mass to remove references to it being a sacrifice. Ulrich Zwingli ensured that relics, paintings, decorations, ornaments, and vestments were removed from church buildings. Martin Bucer is credited with introducing an early form of the regulative principle in arguing that corporate worship should be conducted according to Scripture, thus removing extra-biblical ceremonies and rituals. These actions, and others like them, reformed corporate worship in at least five ways.[7]

First, Scripture became central to corporate worship. This makes perfect sense given our treatment of *Sola Scriptura* earlier in this book. If Scripture is the final authority for the individual Christian, the logical step is to let it control corporate worship. In order to make Scripture central the Reformers ensured that corporate worship was conducted in the common language of the people to aid comprehension. Scripture was also read aloud in the common language and preaching became expository as consecutive texts were both explained and applied book by book and week by week.

Second, the congregation participated in corporate worship. Undoubtedly, this was in part due to corporate worship being conducted in the common language of the people. Whether by intention or simply a result of the way the medieval church conducted their services, the congregation were largely spectators. Driven by the Reformation cry of *Soli Deo Gloria*, this changed under the influence of the Reformers. The noted historian, Roland Bainton, claimed that Martin Luther should be considered the father of congregational singing.[8] There was certainly a significant shift away from the performance of instrumental compositions to the congregation singing with one voice. In addition to congregational participation in song, the congregation were also invited to partake of both the bread and wine at communion. Previously they had been refused the wine.

Third, the sacraments were restored to their biblical simplicity. The Reformers argued: "If the sacraments are to edify they must be understood. In order to be understood they must be accompanied with biblical exposition and conducted with biblical simplicity."[9] As noted above, Martin Luther made this move by revising the existing liturgy for Mass. Furthermore, the Reformers removed five of the medieval church's seven sacraments, leaving only baptism and communion.

Fourth, there was a renewed appreciation of and focus on the work of the Holy Spirit. In the medieval church the external features of corporate worship had assumed priority. The Reformers desired to direct attention away from the external towards the internal, notably by focusing on the work of the Spirit in the Christian. One practical way in which this was accomplished was by interspersing the corporate worship service with prayer. By this practice, the Reformers subtly communicated and demonstrated their utter dependence on the Holy Spirit's work in the life of the congregation.

Fifth, the internal architecture of the church was altered. For the Reformers, and their first converts, the most notably change was the replacing of the altar with a table. Communion was no longer served from an altar, as a sacrifice would be, but from a table, as a meal would be. The Reformers also moved the pulpit to take centre stage, thus communicating the centrality of Scripture in the life of the congregation. Indeed, church buildings became less ostentatious. Although it took time, church buildings eventually became much simpler. A noticeable feature from within the Baptist tradition, of which I am a part.

The Reformation cry of *Soli Deo Gloria* clearly reformed the sphere of corporate worship. Yet, it is significant that it not only altered the theory, but the practice. If God alone was to be given all the glory, one did not just need to think differently, but also act differently.

Church Government

The second sphere of life to be reformed by the thinking inherent in *Soli Deo Gloria* was church government. It must be conceded that this change developed at a much slower rate. Even so, the way individual congregations and groupings of congregations were governed was slowly reformed. For example, despite Martin Luther maintaining the episcopal system of church government, he reinterpreted the function and authority of Bishops. A more significant shift occurred in 1541, when John Calvin published his Ecclesiastical Ordinances. This material, evidently influenced by Martin Bucer's vision of the church, eventually gave rise to the system that now governs the Presbyterian Church.[10]

As a Baptist, I would contend that in this aspect the Reformation did not go far enough. Rather than authority remaining outside of a congregation in a presbytery or a Bishop, I would argue that Scripture presents a picture of individual congregations governing themselves while working in partnership. Nevertheless, it is undeniable that a positive trajectory was set in motion during the Reformation regarding church government. Indeed, to a much greater degree congregations began to participate in the appointment of their leaders and the governing of their congregational life.

Family Life

The third sphere in which reform was driven by *Soli Deo Gloria* was family life. It was not simply church life that was impacted by the theology of the Reformation. Theology "came home" with the Reformers and raised the honour and dignity of marriage. The Reformers directly challenged the perceived superiority of celibacy and championed both marriage and family life. This was particularly apparent in the former monk, Martin Luther, marrying the former nun, Katherine von Bora, in 1525. Family life, as it was to be promoted by the Reformers, took on three particular aspects.

First, the Reformers promoted marriage. To many, marriage was a necessity to control particular desires, but to the Reformers marriage offered a rich companionship between two people. John Calvin exemplified this in tender words after the death of his wife: "I have been bereaved of the best companion of my life."[11] This focus on companionship was developed by those who stood in the shadow of the Reformation. Commenting on Genesis 2:22, Mathew Henry wrote:

> The woman was made out of a rib out of the side of Adam; not made out of his head to top him, nor made out of his feet to be trampled upon by him, but out of his side to be equal with him, under his arm to be protected, and near his heart to be beloved.

The Reformers were not cold, heartless, theology machines. They were human beings who recognised the great gift and precious companionship of a spouse.

Second, the Reformers upheld the God-ordained gift of sexual relations within the marriage relationship. Prevailing sixteenth century thought was that celibacy and sexual abstinence promoted a godlier spirituality. Sexual intercourse was understood to be bad but desirable, and this is reflected in the literature of the era. In direct conflict with the prevailing understanding, the Reformers contended that sexual intimacy was a gift from God to be enjoyed (particularly by the people of God) in the way that God had prescribed. By doing so, "the Reformers affirmed the goodness of sexual relations and even sexual pleasure in marriage."[12]

Third, the Reformers also devoted attention to family life. To some degree this was inevitable, given the common consequence of sexual relations is the conception of children. In particular, the Reformers developed a high view of children and the task of raising them. The nuclear family as the foundation of western society is a result of the Reformers' high view of family life. As Terry Johnson observes: "The greatest service that one could perform for humanity was to rear godly children."[13]

Society at Large

The fourth sphere of life to be impacted by the Reformation cry of *Soli Deo Gloria* was society at large. One of the notable features of the Reformation was that it did not simply benefit Protestant Christians. Rather, it benefited all of society in a variety of ways. This was noted to some degree in chapter one, as we were introduced to the power and beauty of Scripture as it transformed Geneva. There are two additional ways in which the Reformation reformed society at large.

First, society benefited from the Reformers' significant emphasis on education. Indispensable to the cause of the Reformation was the literacy of the populace. Martin Luther explained: "The Scripture cannot be understood without the languages, the languages can be learned only in school."[14] In fact, as early as 1523 Luther was arguing for compulsory education for all children. John Calvin maintained this emphasis by establishing the Geneva Academy in 1559. The Academy developed into one of the world's foremost universities, evidencing a concern for broad-based and quality education that has been a hallmark of Protestantism, and especially Reformed Protestantism. Terry Johnson concludes: "The Reformation was the best friend that education ever had. Learning is a good thing, the Protestant tradition continues to say, to be pursued to the glory of God."[15]

Second, society benefited from the impact of the Reformation in the political sphere. Neither Martin Luther nor John Calvin fully developed the political implications of their theologies. Nevertheless, their successors did. Groupings such as the Puritans, France's Huguenots, Holland's "Beggars", and Scotland's Covenanters, and individuals such as John Cotton, John Locke, Thomas Hooker, Thomas Shepard, John Davenport, and Richard Mather all developed the political implications of Reformation thinking. Thus, thanks in no small part to the Reformation cry of *Soli Deo Gloria*, the political landscape began to look very different across Europe. Among the most pertinent developments were:

A. *The separation of Church and state* – no longer could the state dictate how the Church should function, and no longer could the Church dictate how the state should function. The era of theocracy was over; Church and state were no longer one and the same.

B. *Governmental responsibility to resist tyrants* – the state government possessed both the ability and responsibility to enforce the rule of law. In doing so, good behaviour was to be encouraged and bad behaviour curbed (Rom. 13:1–5). Ultimately, tyrants were to be resisted by the state.

C. *Equality of humanity* – race wars continued to be waged across Europe and further afield for many years to come, but the Reformers argued for the equality of humanity. In the Reformers' thinking humanity stood on an equal footing before God in both grace and sin. The political implication was the equality of humanity in society.

D. *Freedom of conscience* – in accordance with Scripture, no individual should be forced to go against his conscience. There should be religious freedom and toleration, including the freedom to gather for worship (no matter what theological outlook that particular grouping possessed) and freedom of speech.

The impact of the Reformation on the political sphere is apparent. Many of the rights and freedoms that individuals possess in western democracies can be clearly discerned in these immediate implications of Reformation thinking. Modern societies and their freedoms are, to a large degree, God's gift to humanity through the Reformers and their successors.

Soli Deo Gloria?[16]

You could be forgiven if the question rattling around your head at this point is: "What exactly has all of this human effort got to do with *Soli Deo Gloria*?" It may appear to you that this exploration of reform in every sphere simply highlights gifted individuals who applied themselves appropriately. Yet, if we were to place the Reformers on a pedestal and glory in their ingenuity, we would be in error.

The aim in documenting the reform that reached into every sphere of life is to display the extent to which the Reformers believed that God must be served and worshipped. The Reformation distinguished itself from other movements by the core understanding that all things must be undertaken in a manner that glorifies God alone. For the Reformers it did not matter whether one was preparing a weighty sermon or feeding a hungry child, the motivation for that action had to be the glory of God alone. *Soli Deo Gloria* must be the motivation in every sphere of life. Thus, corporate worship, church government, family life, and society at large must be engaged with the desire of glorifying God alone.

Terry Johnson claims: "The Reformation, in its zeal to pursue the glory of God in all of life, had much to do with giving the world its modern form."[17] It is undoubtedly true that many other events and periods throughout history have left an indelible mark on our modern societies. The Reformation, however, by its simple yet demanding cry of *Soli Deo Gloria* brought about reform in every sphere of life.

Soli Deo Gloria in Scripture

The Glory of the Holy One of Israel in Isaiah

The book of Isaiah can be a difficult book to comprehend given its massive size and the fact that it spans decades of human history.[18] Isaiah is addressing the people of God as they face the threat of exile, experience exile, and eagerly await return from exile. The prophet explains, "the exile will show that God is incomparable: there is no God like him, able to explain the past – Creator; able to tell the future – Lord; able to do a brand new thing – Redeemer."[19] This incomparableness is effectively communicated by Isaiah with his favoured title for God: The Holy One of Israel. It could be argued that the central theme of the book of Isaiah is God himself, and how all things relate to him. God's glory appears to be a primary concern throughout the book, indeed throughout human history.

Within the book of Isaiah the Holy One of Israel repeatedly declares that particular things are made or done for his glory. This is observed in Isaiah 43. God seeks to teach his people that He alone will be their Saviour; no-one else is capable of rescuing Israel. Therefore, He calls them to fear not (vv. 1, 5). The Holy One of Israel will protect them (v. 2) and gather them again from the nations (v. 4–6). In verse 7, it is made explicit that only God's people will enjoy this salvation, but also present is the grand purpose of God's people and his saving acts – namely, God's glory. God's people are created, formed, and made for God's glory (v. 7). This is the climax of the introduction to Isaiah 43. The Holy One of Israel created and formed a people for his glory, and in a display of that glory he will now protect and rescue them. The people of God are made for God's glory alone.

In Isaiah 48 God acts for His glory alone. As Gary Smith notes, "God originally created the world and the nation of Israel to bring glory to himself."[20] That was the thrust of Isaiah 43:7, and yet by chapter 48 this no longer appears to be the case. The nation of Israel is attempting to confess the name of God, but they are not doing it correctly (v. 1). Rather, the people are showing their utter stubbornness by crediting the glorious acts of the Holy One of Israel to mere idols (vv. 4–5). In response God acts for His glory; He brings restrained affliction on His people (vv. 9–10). Israel were not being true to their God, but He was certain to be true to himself. God acts for His glory alone: "For my own sake, for my own sake, I do it, for how should my name be profaned? My glory I will not give to another" (v. 11). Gary Smith explains:

> In the end God will not allow his name to be profaned by sinful and rebellious people. They must either be judged or transformed...How can God allow his majestic glory to be diminished in any way? How could God ever allow people to give his praise and glory to another? These rhetorical questions indicate that the mere suggestion of such an idea is unthinkable. It will never happen because a holy God of immeasurable glory cannot go against his nature. He is holy and glorious; nothing will happen that might call into question his essence or impinge on his majestic reputation.[21]

God's people were made to bring Him glory, this glory belongs to Him and Him alone. If there is any danger this glory will be granted to another the Holy One of Israel will act, and in Isaiah 48 He does.

Isaiah 61 rounds out the picture for us as we see God glorifying Himself not through affliction, but through abundant blessing. In the closing section of his prophecy, Isaiah casts a glorious vision of the Holy One of Israel's coming kingdom. It is a kingdom in which God will bestow abundant blessing on His people. Isaiah 61 opens with the proclamation of the year of the LORD's favour in which good news will be proclaimed to the poor. In that era the broken-hearted will be comforted, the captive will experience liberty, mourning will be exchanged for praise, and God's people will be named righteous (vv. 1–3). This act of God is an expanded echo of Isaiah 60:21 as the purpose clause at the end of 61:3 makes clear. God has acted again, in blessing, that He may be glorified.

The Reformers argued and lived with the conviction that every sphere of life pertained to God's glory. Their deep desire was to give God the glory and honour He is due – and to give it to Him alone. Our brief survey of some passages in Isaiah suggests that the Reformers were correct in their inclinations. The Holy One of Israel Himself, through the prophet Isaiah, declares *Soli Deo Gloria*.

The Glory of the Holy One of Israel in the Church

The declaration of *Soli Deo Gloria* by God in Isaiah is applied to the Church in 1 Corinthians 10:31: "So, whether you eat or drink, or whatever you do, do all to the glory of God."

First Corinthians is a letter written by Paul to a church established under his ministry while in Corinth. The Church was struggling; it appeared to be suffering from similar symptoms to Israel in Isaiah 43. The Corinthian Church was replete with one-upmanship, sexual immorality, divisions, drunkenness, and, unsurprisingly considering the above, disorderly worship. Paul writes to this messy scenario in an attempt to correct their errors and apparently answer their questions. Towards the end of a section detailing the appropriate actions concerning food offered to idols and forgoing one's rights for the good of the corporate body, Paul commands the Church to glorify God in all things (10:31).

With this verse in view John MacArthur writes: "Paul is saying that even in the most mundane, routine, nonspiritual things of life, like ordinary eating and drinking, God is to be glorified. His glory is to be our life commitment."[22] I take issue with John MacArthur's use of "nonspiritual", but the sentiment is accurate. *Soli Deo Gloria* is to be the Corinthians' aim in all things, from the most prestigious act to that which is perfectly ordinary. It is another simple biblical command to understand, and yet ever so difficult to be obedient to. Nevertheless,

> The highest purpose any individual can have is to be totally absorbed in the person of God, and to view all of life through eyes filled with His wonder and glory. That is the perspective of the true worshipper, the one who truly glorifies God.[23]

Isaiah repeatedly communicates to his reader that God's glory is God's supreme concern. Paul, in 1 Corinthians, applies this principle by arguing it should be the Christian's supreme concern.[24] This is not some abstract concept, however. It is concrete—eating, drinking, or indeed anything, should be done for the glory of God alone. *Soli Deo Gloria,* according to God Himself, is to be the controlling factor in all our living. There is no abstract goal to living life in this manner; Paul gives the Corinthian Church this command for God's glory and their good. "In short, Paul encourages us to glorify God in all things by seeking the good of others, for the ultimate goal of seeing people saved and the church strengthened."[25]

Soli Deo Gloria Today

Knowing God

There is an arrogance in modern Christianity. Too few Christians devote an appropriate amount of time to knowing God through the means He has appointed. We assume that we can know our God by merely singing a few songs on a Sunday morning and making it through a sermon once a week. This betrays an arrogance; we presume we know all we need to know about our God. Yet, the God of the Bible is beyond our full comprehension (Isa. 55:8–9; Rom. 11:34–35). There is always something more to know about God.

One of the reasons that the Reformation cry of *Soli Deo Gloria* held a vital and controlling position in the thinking of the Reformers was their grand and glorious vision of who God is. Therefore, they devoted their lives to growing in the knowledge of God (2 Peter 3:18). At only 20 years of age, Charles Spurgeon asserted:

> The highest science, the loftiest speculation, the mightiest philosophy, which can ever engage the attention of a child of God, is the name, the nature, the person, the work, the doings, and the existence of the great God whom he calls his Father.[26]

Charles Spurgeon had captured the motivation of the Reformers. Serious thinking about God leads to a larger vision of who He is. The reality is that we will never be enthused to give glory alone to God if we do not understand Him for who He truly is.

Serving God

Closely related to the issue of knowing God is that of serving God. The Reformation cry of *Soli Deo Gloria* provokes piercing questions about our motivation. *Why* do we do certain things? The reality is that the motivation for many of our actions is our own glory. We seek to be adored, desired, and honoured above all others. Essentially, we seek to be glorified.

Corporate worship is a wonderful weapon in destroying this self-glorification. David VanDrunen explains:

> The fact that worship is an immensely unproductive activity from an earthly perspective provides a helpful reminder that *Soli Deo Gloria* is really not about our own achievements: God most delights to glorify himself through us when we rest from our seemingly productive labours and call upon his name in truth.[27]

To partake in activities such as corporate worship is an effective reminder that we should be serving God. There is only One who should be adored, desired, and honoured above all others. Setting time aside from courting favour, earning money, and making a name for ourselves recalibrates our propensity to self-glorification. In corporate worship, we are reminded that God's favour towards us is most important; we are reminded that everything belongs to God and we are merely stewarding it; and, we are reminded that glory should be ascribed to His name alone, not to us (Ps. 115:1). Our motivation should be serving God because glory belongs to Him alone.

Living for God

The most striking thing about the Reformers' presentation of *Soli Deo Gloria* is that they effectively removed the religious and secular divide that was so entrenched in sixteenth century society. In both their thinking and practice the Reformers contended that all of life should be lived to the glory of God alone. We must recapture this impetus today.

Contemporary Christianity may assent to this verbally, but I am unconvinced that we truly believe it. For the Reformers, pastors and missionaries were no more likely to glorify God than the housewives and teachers. Full-time employment in Christian service is a blessing, and vitally important, but so is serving others by offering medical help or generating a healthy economy. Devotion to studying Scripture and teaching its truths to others is a crucial ministry, but likewise feeding our children and paying our taxes is vital to a vibrant Christian witness.

The Reformers removed the wedge between the so-called secular and religious domains of life in the sixteenth century. We stand in their legacy and in doing so we must not let this division return. It is truly remarkable that the theology of the Reformers not only brought the gospel of Jesus Christ to the fore again, but also provided better education, fairer government, and increased welfare for those in need. Today our theology must do likewise; it must propel us forward into the world in such a way that our light shines before all men, so they may see our good works and glorify our Father in heaven (Matt. 5:16).

Conclusion: All of Life

Greg Strawbridge excellently captures the thrust of the argument made in this chapter:

> In contrast to the monastic division of life into sacred versus secular perpetuated by [the] Roman Church, the [R]eformers saw all of life to be lived under the Lordship of Christ. Every activity of the Christian is to be sanctified unto the glory of God. [28]

It is incumbent upon us to follow their lead. We must recognise that all of life is to be lived to the glory of God alone, and thus give God the glory He rightly demands and is due.

CONCLUSION

Remaining Faithful in the Twenty-First Century

Over five hundred years ago, God raised up a generation of Christians who argued with conviction that Scripture alone is the Church's final authority. In accepting Scripture alone as the Church's final authority, they proceeded to explain that salvation is by grace alone, through faith alone, in Christ alone. God has acted of His own accord to rescue his people from their sin. All we can do, contended the Reformers, is trust and that trust must be placed in the person and work of Jesus Christ alone. Consequently, there can be no other response to these truths than the conviction that all of life is to be lived to the glory of this good God alone.

In the centuries both preceding and succeeding the Reformation, the health of the Christian Church has both struggled and flourished. When it seems that the Church is nearing extinction, God raises up another generation of Christians who stand firm. Yet, when the Church appears triumphant, it is prone to lapsing into error. This struggling and flourishing often takes place simultaneously across the globe. As the Church experiences resurgence in one location, it is battling error in another. The danger, I believe, is found in a neglect of the truths we have explored in this book.

The Church lapses into error and faces extinction when it fails to submit itself to Scripture as the final authority. Naturally, this leads to a misshapen understanding of salvation in Jesus Christ and a worldview in which God is not afforded all the glory. On the other hand, the Church is resurgent and triumphant when it humbly submits to Scripture as its final authority. Unsurprisingly, this attitude of humility results in a gospel proclamation that makes it clear that God initiated, accomplished, and applied salvation's plan. In light of such majestic grace, the Church is then compelled to live a life in which all of the glory is God's alone.

Today, our prayer must be that we do not lose these truths. It is imperative that we contend for the truth that was once for all delivered to the saints (Jude 3). The Church today must continually submit under the final authority of Scripture alone. It must continue to wrestle with the tension of God's sovereignty and man's responsibility in salvation. But more than this, these truths must trickle from our heads to our hearts. The truths that re-emerged in sixteenth century Europe must inform and impact both our life and our theology. If they do, we will be compelled to proclaim the gospel of Jesus Christ in all its fullness and glory no matter the personal cost.

We are products of our past. Whether or not the *Five Solas* have been a part of your past to date does not matter, because they can be now. As these Reformation truths shape us in the present, we stand indebted to previous generations who have blessed us with a godly legacy. Now we must ask ourselves what legacy we will leave for future generations? Will these tremendous truths be evident in our lives and theology, or will we force a later generation to re-discover them? Our prayer must be that we will be men and women who remain faithful in the twenty-first century for the benefit of future generations and the glory of God alone.

END NOTES

Introduction

1   Stephen J. Wellum, 'Solus Christus: What the Reformers Taught and Why It Still Matters', *Southern Baptist Journal of Theology* 19, no. 4 (2015): 5–6.

Chapter 1 - Sola Scriptura

1   This introduction is based heavily on the account presented in James Montgomery Boice, *Whatever Happened to the Gospel of Grace? Rediscovering the Doctrines That Shook the World* (Wheaton: Crossway, 2009), 83–84.
2   For more on this development see Keith A. Mathison, 'Sola Scriptura', in *After Darkness, Light: Essays in Honour of R. C. Sproul*, ed. R. C. Sproul Jr. (Phillipsburg: P&R Publishing, 2003), 34.
3   For more detail on these three debates see Matthew Barrett, 'Sola Scriptura in the Strange Land of Evangelicalism: The Peculiar but Necessary Responsibility of Defending Sola Scriptura Against Our Own Kind', *Southern Baptist Journal of Theology* 19, no. 4 (2015): 11–16.
4   The historian is Harold Grimm. Quoted in Barrett, 12.
5   As quoted in Barrett, 18
6   Boice, *Whatever Happened to the Gospel of Grace?*, 66.
7   On this see Peter A. Lillback and Richard B. Gaffin Jr, eds., *Thy Word Is Still Truth: Essential Writings on the Doctrine of Scripture from the Reformation to Today* (Phillipsburg: P&R Publishing, 2013), 10. I want to thank Edwin Ewart for bringing this insight to my attention in a magazine article in abcInsight.
8   As quoted in Lillback and Gaffin Jr, 78.
9   Barrett, 'Sola Scriptura', 14.
10   John MacArthur, 'What Does Sola Scriptura Mean?', *Ligonier* (blog), 2015, https://www.ligonier.org/blog/what-does-sola-scriptura-mean/.
11   MacArthur.
12   Mathison, 'Sola Scriptura', 46–47.
13   Peter C. Craigie, *Deuteronomy*, The New International Commentary on the Old Testament (Grand Rapids: Eerdmans, 1976), 185. Craigie writes: 'The wilderness tested and disciplined the people in various ways. On the one hand, the desolation of the wilderness removed the natural props and supports which man by nature depends on; it cast the people back on God, who alone could provide the strength to survive the wilderness.'
14   Meredith G. Kline, *Treaty of the Great King: The Covenant Structure of Deuteronomy* (Grand Rapids: Eerdmans Publishing Company, 1963), 71.
15   For more on this theme see Daniel I. Block, *Deuteronomy*, The NIV

Application Commentary (Grand Rapids: Zondervan, 2012), 228.
16   Tremper Longman III and Raymond B. Dillard, *An Introduction to the Old Testament*, Second Edition (Nottingham: Inter-Varsity Press, 2007), 116. Emphasis added.
17   This point of view is further strengthened by reading πειρασθηωαι as 'test' rather than 'temptation'. Both translations are legitimate.
18   For more on this see the discussion in Donald A. Carson, *The Expositor's Bible Commentary: Matthew*, Revised, vol. 9 (Grand Rapids: Zondervan, 2010), 139–41.
19   Carson, 9:141–42.
20   For the insights in this paragraph I am indebted to Leon Morris, *The Gospel According to Matthew*, The Pillar New Testament Commentary (Leicester: Apollos, 1992), 74.
21   Kevin DeYoung, *Taking God at His Word: Why the Bible Is Worth Knowing, Trusting and Loving* (Nottingham: Inter-Varsity Press, 2014), 54–55. This is an excellent introduction to the doctrine of Scripture. Both brief and accessible; highly recommended.
22   DeYoung, 55.
23   Terry L. Johnson, *The Case for Traditional Protestantism: The Solas of the Reformation* (Edinburgh: Banner of Truth, 2013), 31.
24   Alister McGrath quoted in Mathison, 'Sola Scriptura', 37.
25   Edwin Ewart, 'Sola Scriptura', *Abcinsight*, 2017, 13.
26   See Barrett, 'Sola Scriptura', 11.
27   Boice, *Whatever Happened to the Gospel of Grace?*, 79.
28   Johnson, *Traditional Protestantism*, 25.

Chapter 2 - Sola Gratia

1   This introduction is based on information gleaned from James I. Packer and O. R. Johnson, 'Historical and Theological Introduction', in *The Bondage of the Will: A New Translation* (Cambridge: James Clarke, 1957).
2   Michael Horton, 'Sola Gratia', in *After Darkness, Light: Essays in Honour of R. C. Sproul*, ed. R. C. Sproul Jr. (Phillipsburg: P&R Publishing, 2003), 112.
3   Edwin Ewart, 'Sola Gratia', *Abcinsight*, 2017, 28.
4   Packer and Johnson, 'Historical and Theological Introduction', 25.
5   Quoted in Packer and Johnson, 48.
6   Packer and Johnson, 48.
7   For more on this see Carl R. Trueman, 'The Word as a Means of Grace', *Southern Baptist Journal of Theology* 19, no. 4 (2015): especially 61.
8   Packer and Johnson, 'Historical and Theological Introduction', 40.
9   Also, Packer and Johnson, 40. The other work was the little children's Catechism.
10   Horton, 'Sola Gratia', 121. Emphasis added.
11   Charles Finney, *Systematic Theology*, Lecture XXVII - Regeneration http://www.ccel.org/ccel/finney/theology.iv.xxvi.html. Accessed 03/09/2018.
12   Ewart, 'Sola Gratia', 28. The quotation is taken from Matthew Barrett, *Reformation Theology*, 2017.
13   See Block, *Deuteronomy*, 206-7 for a defence of this argument.
14   For more on this see Kline, *Treaty of the Great King*, 68.
15   Block, *Deuteronomy*, 39.

16   Rather than using the colder terminology of *goy*, Moses use the warmer term *'am*.
17   For more on the Hebrew term and its uniqueness see Block, *Deuteronomy*, 209-10, and, Craigie, *Deuteronomy*, 179.
18   On this see Block, Deuteronomy, 210-11. It will also be noted that the fourfold division of verses 7-8 expressed above is indebted to Block's treatment of the same.
19   I came across this quote in the nineteenth century commentator Johann Peter Lange's commentary which was accessed via BibleWorks.
20   This quote was accessed via BibleWorks.
21   Johnson, *Traditional Protestantism*, 15.
22   William W. Klein, 'Ephesians', in *The Expositor's Bible Commentary*, ed. Tremper Longman III and David E. Garland, Revised (Grand Rapids: Zondervan, 2006), 64-65.
23   Klein, 63.
24   John R. W. Stott, *The Bible Speaks Today: The Message of Ephesians* (Leicester: Inter-Varsity Press, 1979), 81-82.
25   Peter T. O'Brien, *The Pillar New Testament Commentary: The Letter to the Ephesians* (Leicester: Apollos, 1999), 175-76.
26   Klyne Snodgrass, *The NIV Application Commentary: Ephesians* (Grand Rapids: Zondervan, 1996), 103.
27   Stott, *BST: Ephesians*, 83.
28   My thinking on application was greatly aided by the suggestions in Ewart, 'Sola Gratia'.
29   Boice, *Whatever Happened to the Gospel of Grace?*, 107.
30   Johnson, *Traditional Protestantism*, 108.
31   Ewart, 'Sola Gratia', 29.
32   Quoted in Trueman, 'The Word as a Means of Grace', 67-68.
33   Trueman, 75-76.
34   Ewart, 'Sola Gratia', 29.
35   Packer and Johnson, 'Historical and Theological Introduction', 59.
36   See Johnson, *Traditional Protestantism*, 122. He writes: 'Is the battle-cry of sola gratia still relevant? Yes it is! Martin Luther was indeed right. It is the "hinge on which all turns." If the doors of self-righteousness are to remain barred; if we are to resist the seductions of the religious systems of merit; if salvation is to remain free to us as God's gift; if God alone is to receive all glory, then sola gratia is as important today as it has ever been.'

Chapter 3 - Sola Fide

1   The introduction is compiled from the accounts of Martin Luther's conversion recorded in Boice, *Whatever Happened to the Gospel of Grace?*, 132-33, and, Johnson, *Traditional Protestantism*, 3-6.
2   For a superb biography on Martin Luther I recommend, Roland H. Bainton, *Here I Stand: A Life of Martin Luther* (Peabody: Hendrickson Publishers, 2009).
3   Thomas R. Schreiner, 'Justification by Works and Sola Fide', *Southern Baptist Journal of Theology* 19, no. 4 (2015): 40.
4   Sinclair B. Ferguson, 'Sola Fide', in *After Darkness, Light: Essays in Honour of R. C. Sproul*, ed. R. C. Sproul Jr. (Phillipsburg: P&R Publishing, 2003), 85.

5   For more on this see the discussion in Ferguson, 84–85.
6   Johnson, *Traditional Protestantism*, 96.
7   Johnson, 97.
8   Boice, *Whatever Happened to the Gospel of Grace?*, 130.
9   Quoted in Boice, 130.
10 Quoted in Johnson, *Traditional Protestantism*, 94.
11 Quoted in Boice, *Whatever Happened to the Gospel of Grace?*, 130.
12 John Calvin quoted in Johnson, *Traditional Protestantism*, 76.
13 Quoted in Ferguson, 'Sola Fide', 93.
14 See Ferguson, 82 for these quotes from Calvin.
15 Quoted in Boice, *Whatever Happened to the Gospel of Grace?*, 148.
16 Cranmer's quotations can be found in Boice, 130.
17 Quoted in Boice, 130.
18 Boice, 137.
19 Ferguson, 'Sola Fide', 84.
20 Boice, *Whatever Happened to the Gospel of Grace?*, 137.
21 Quoted in Boice, 139.
22 Quoted in Boice, 140.
23 James K. Bruckner, *The NIV Application Commentary: Jonah, Nahum, Habakkuk, Zephaniah* (Grand Rapids: Zondervan, 2004), 203.
24 Either of the terms Chaldean or Babylonian can be employed in this context and refer to the same nation.
25 O. Palmer Robertson, *The New International Commentary on the Old Testament: The Books of Nahum, Habakkuk, and Zephaniah* (Grand Rapids: Eerdmans, 1990), 174.
26 Robertson, 181.
27 Robertson, 183.
28 Leon Morris, *The Epistle to the Romans* (Leicester: Inter-Varsity Press, 1988), 173.
29 John R. W. Stott, *The Bible Speaks Today: The Message of Romans*, Reprint (Nottingham: Inter-Varsity Press, 2012), 108.
30 *ESV: Study Bible* (Wheaton: Crossway, 2008), 2163.
31 Douglas J. Moo, *The NIV Application Commentary: Romans* (Grand Rapids: Zondervan, 2000), 135.
32 Morris, *Romans*, 193.
33 This structure is explained and defended in Thomas R. Schreiner, *Baker Exegetical Commentary on the New Testament: Romans* (Grand Rapids: Baker Academic, 1998), 210.
34 Schreiner, 212.
35 Mark Dever, *The Message of the New Testament* (Wheaton: Crossway, 2005), 154..
36 Morris, *Romans*, 209
37 Schreiner, *BECNT: Romans*, 241.
38 Stott, *BST: Romans*, 117.
39 Moo, *NIVAC: Romans*, 164.
40 An excellent book on the topic is John Piper, *Think: The Life of the Mind and the Love of God* (Nottingham: Inter-Varsity Press, 2010).
41 Ferguson, 'Sola Fide', 91.
42 Johnson, *Traditional Protestantism*, 78.
43 Quoted in Piper, *Think*, 70.

Chapter 4 - Solus Christus

1   This introduction is adapted from the material in Boice, *Whatever Happened to the Gospel of Grace?*, 93–94.
2   Wellum, 'Solus Christus', 83.
3   Wellum, 83.
4   For more on this see, Johnson, *Traditional Protestantism*, 8; Wellum, 'Solus Christus', 83–84.
5   James I. Packer, *Honouring the People of God: The Collected Shorter Writings of J. I. Packer*, 4 (Carlisle: Paternoster Press, 1999), 7.
6   Quoted in Boice, Whatever Happened to the Gospel of Grace?, 95.
7   See, Boice, 89.
8   Quoted in Edwin Ewart, 'Solus Christus', *Abcinsight*, 2017, 22.
9   Quoted in Johnson, *Traditional Protestantism*, 74.
10   Quoted in Ewart, 'Solus Christus', 23.
11   Quoted in Ewart, 23.
12   Quoted in Wellum, 'Solus Christus', 84.
13   Cf. the discussion in Wellum, 82–83.
14   Ewart, 'Solus Christus', 22.
15   Ewart, 23.
16   Johnson, *Traditional Protestantism*, 68.
17   Johnson, 63.
18   For more on this see Wellum, 'Solus Christus', 84.
19   John H. Armstrong quoted in Johnson, *Traditional Protestantism*, 47.
20   Derek Kidner, *Tyndale Old Testament Commentaries: Genesis* (London: Tyndale Press, 1967), 70.
21   John H. Sailhamer, 'Genesis', in *The Expositor's Bible Commentary*, ed. Tremper Longman III and David E. Garland, Revised, vol. 1 (Grand Rapids: Zondervan, 2008), 91.
22   Sailhamer, 91.
23   In favour of this view are James Dixon, *Genesis: Expository Thoughts* (Darlington: Evangelical Press, 2005), 95; Kidner, *TOTC: Genesis*, 71.
24   For a magnificent treatment of this so-called 'Servant Song' see J. Alec Motyer, '"Stricken for the Transgression of My People": The Atoning Work of Isaiah's Suffering Servant', in *From Heaven He Came and Sought Her: Definite Atonement in Historical, Biblical, Theological, and Pastoral Perspective*, ed. David Gibson and Jonathan Gibson (Wheaton: Crossway, 2013).
25   John R. W. Stott, *The Bible Speaks Today: The Message of Acts* (Nottingham: Inter-Varsity Press, 1990), 97.
26   Philip G. Ryken, *Reformed Expository Commentary: Galatians* (Phillipsburg: P&R Publishing, 2005), 22.
27   Thomas R. Schreiner, *Biblical Theology for Christian Proclamation: Commentary on Hebrews* (Nashville: B&H Publishing, 2015), 455.
28   Schreiner, 455.
29   Boice, *Whatever Happened to the Gospel of Grace?*, 105.
30   John MacArthur, 'Solus Christus', in *After Darkness, Light: Essays in Honour of R. C. Sproul*, ed. R. C. Sproul Jr. (Phillipsburg: P&R Publishing, 2003), 152, 154.
31   MacArthur, 154.
32   Boice, *Whatever Happened to the Gospel of Grace?*, 88.

Chapter 5 - Soli Deo Gloria

1   The introduction is based in part on Johnson, *Traditional Protestantism*, 15–16. Also consult Foxe's *Book of Martyrs*.
2   Johnson, 16.
3   Boice, *Whatever Happened to the Gospel of Grace?*, 152.
4   See the introductory remarks in David VanDrunen, 'Glory to God Alone: Another Look at a Reformation Sola', *Southern Baptist Journal of Theology* 19, no. 4 (2015): 109.
5   Edwin Ewart, 'Soli Deo Gloria', *Abcinsight*, 2017, 16.
6   Johnson, *Traditional Protestantism*, 125.
7   For an expansion on the following five aspects of corporate worship see Johnson, 126–43.
8   Bainton, *Here I Stand*, 344.
9   Johnson, *Traditional Protestantism*, 129.
10 Willem van't Spijker, 'Bucer's influence on Calvin: church and community' in David F. Wright (ed.), *Martin Bucer: Reforming Church and Community* (Cambridge: Cambridge University Press,1994),32ff.
11 Quoted in Johnson, *Traditional Protestantism*, 147.
12 Johnson, 148.
13 Johnson, 149.
14 Quoted in Johnson, 151.
15 Johnson, 154.
16 This conclusion is aided by concepts conveyed in R. C. Sproul Jr., 'Soli Deo Gloria', in *After Darkness, Light: Essays in Honour of R. C. Sproul* (Phillipsburg: P&R Publishing, 2003), 191.
17 Johnson, *Traditional Protestantism*, 162.
18 For an accessible overview see S. D. Ellison, *The Holy One of Israel: Exploring Isaiah* (Independently Published, 2019).
19 John N. Oswalt, *New International Commentary on the Old Testament: Isaiah 40–66* (Grand Rapids: Eerdmans Publishing Company, 1998), 9.
20 Gary V. Smith, *New American Commentary: Isaiah 40-66* (Nashville: B&H Publishing, 2009), 196.
21 Smith, 324.
22 John MacArthur, *The MacArthur New Testament Commentary: 1 Corinthians* (Chicago: Moody Publishers, 1984), 248.
23 MacArthur, 244.
24 MacArthur, 248. He writes: 'God's glory is His supreme concern and should also be our supreme concern.'
25 VanDrunen, 'Glory to God Alone: Another Look at a Reformation Sola', 126.
26 Quoted in Boice, *Whatever Happened to the Gospel of Grace?*, 150.
27 VanDrunen, 'Glory to God Alone: Another Look at a Reformation Sola', 125.
28 Greg Strawbridge, 'The Five Solas of the Reformation: A Brief Statement', *Reformed Perspectives Magazine* 10, no. 44 (2008).